Women's Voices

The Wisdom of the Grandmothers

4-10-11

To Marlene,
Thank you for being
a wise grandmother willing
to share her light with
others! All the best,
Susan Stark
Christianson

Susan Stark Christianson

D1495919

Library of Congress Control Number: 2010923715
ISBN Number: 978-0-615-35800-0

Walton Group Publications
P.O. Box 20125
Juneau, Alaska 99802, USA

*This book is dedicated to all grandmothers,
mothers, daughters, sisters, aunties,
teachers and friends.*

*In honor of my mother, Mildred Keith Stark,
my grandmothers Toby Noyck Keith and
Anna Bessinger Stark, and my daughters
Joy Christianson Denton and Sarah Christianson.*

*In loving memory of Anisa Michelle Christianson,
James Wilbur Walton, Leonard William Stark,
Kathy Grammer and Marina Panossian Fowles.*

Acknowledgements

Acknowledgement for this project must go to the following:

Jim Walton, whose service provided inspiration, I am forever honored to have been a witness to your life.

Tonya Martynova, Nadia Noeva, and Cheryl Eldemar, who took part in the interviews and filming, I thank you for being part of the journey.

Joy Christianson Denton, Todd Denton and Sarah Christianson, who put up with me and supported my dreams, I am deeply honored to have you in my life.

Millie Stark and Silvia Stoik Christianson, I am humbled by your examples of strength and courage.

Maureen and Gregg Renkes, for your generosity and support, I am forever grateful.

Richard Fowles, Eva Adams and Susana Nino, who helped with healing, guidance and transformation, I am inspired by your encouragement and kindness.

Peggy Brown and Lindsee Acton, whose support made finishing this project possible, I am blessed by your example.

My friends in Juneau and Ojai, your support means more than words can ever say.

Everyone who helped with filming, editing and technical details, especially Margo Waring, Maureen Renkes, Eric Fiederer, and ProWest Video, it couldn't have happened without you.

Maggie, my trusted Magellen GPS, I thank you for allowing me to follow directions, never yelling when you recalculated the route, and for always getting me there.

And to each woman who took the time to share your wisdom and to everyone who reads these words and is touched by them, to you I am most profoundly grateful.

Our Perspective on the World

Table of Content

Prologue

It was snowing the night I drove my Honda CRV onto the M/V Malispina and I was both afraid and full of hope.

"What am I doing, quitting my job, leaving Alaska after almost 25 years to interview grandmothers? Who does such a crazy thing?" Fear of driving on real roads, fear of failure, and fear of not being able to navigate the ramp to get my car onto the ferry came over me like the waves that splashed the ship. It was midnight and I was lined up with about 30 other cars and trucks waiting to head south on the Alaska Marine Highway along the Inside Passage from Alaska's capital to Bellingham, Washington. I couldn't quite shake the idea that living out my lifelong dream might not meet my expectations.

I slowly navigated the car down the long metal ramp and managed to maneuver onto the ship's car deck without hitting anything. I watched as the city lights faded slowly into the distance in my cabin window. The hum of the ship's engine and the slow movement through the water eased my anxiety and the faint glimmer of lights on the water mirrored the glimmer of hope I allowed myself to feel. The Women's Voices Project was launched.

The Women's Voices journey grew out of a dream I had shortly after the death of my mentor and friend from Sitka, Alaska, Tlingit elder Jim Walton. In the dream, I was laying in the sun on a tall tower overlooking Juneau. I realized, after some time, that I didn't want to go back down. At that moment, another tower appeared on a mountain in the woods across the channel separating Juneau from Douglas Island. When I was ready to cross, suddenly a tightrope and a bicycle appeared, connecting the towers.

After riding the bicycle safely across the tightrope to the other side, I looked up to see an approaching storm. Looking down, I saw the lodge in the woods that had been a safe haven in many dreams. For some reason, I lay down on the deck of the second tower and fell asleep. When I awoke within the dream, the storm had passed and I could see the sun coming through the clouds over the distant mountains. I jumped off the tower and began to fly downward, over the tall Sitka Spruce surrounding my lodge. But after circling a few times, I flew back upwards, toward the sun. The next thing I knew I was flying in space, circling the earth, with an incredible sense of joy and oneness with all things.

When I awoke from the dream I knew it had been a message. It was time to finally do what the Creator wanted me to do. It was time to face my fears, leave Juneau, and get started on the project I had long been putting off. It was time to honor Jim Walton's memory.

A Tlingit Elder: A Native Prophesy

At the age of 72, Jim Walton left his family in Alaska and traveled alone, without speaking the Russian language, to Yakutia, an independent republic in Russia's Siberian region. He went in fulfillment of what he said was an Athabaskan elder's prophesy; that someday someone from Alaska would travel back across the land bridge to Siberia to help the Northern indigenous people. In turn, those people would travel back to Alaska to help us. Jim also shared a belief held by many of North America's indigenous peoples that in dark times, the light of wisdom and hope would come from the North.

For years before he went to Yakutia, Jim dedicated his life to helping indigenous people heal from the ravages of alcoholism – a disease that he knew personally all too well. He was the force behind International Cross-Cultural Alcohol Program and was one of the elders who began the Spiritual Unity of Tribes Gatherings in the early 1990s. It was at one of those Gatherings in Nambe Pueblo, New Mexico, that the seeds of the Women's Voices journey were planted in me.

The Gathering, subtitled "Honoring the Grandmothers," was nine days of ceremony, sweat lodges, talking by the sacred fire, healing circles and long days and nights spent camping with hundreds of men, women and children from all across North America. As a young mother, the majority of my days were spent with other women in the make-shift outdoor kitchen, peeling potatoes, cutting vegetables and preparing the food that kept miraculously appearing to feed the thousands who had come to take part. Talk of honoring the grandmothers was ripe on the lips of the men at the Gathering, who seemed to me to be enjoying the fruits of the women's labors. I was disgusted. But as the days of the Gathering went by, I found myself more and more drawn to those who chose to cook and clean. The love and the laughter, the humility and the caring I observed among the women and the young men who helped, was a balm of healing for my empty spirit. How was it that day after day I couldn't find any trace of anger or resentment from these women? How was it that no matter how many hours I worked, or how tired I was, the grandmothers worked longer, laughed harder, and grew more and more joyous as the days went on? I wanted to know their secret.

Jim Walton made his first trip to Siberia to accompany his daughter, Joyce Walton Shales, to a United Nations sponsored event in Yakutsk, the capital of the Sakha Republic, just after the opening of the Soviet Union to the West. When invited to address the conference as a respected elder, Jim told the crowd that the biggest problem they had wasn't the conference's economic or educational focus, it was alcohol. As you might imagine, the response he received was less than warm. But within a year, he returned to Siberia, and made his way to Cherski, the farthest north village in the Republic. Tatyana Martynova, a young psychologist and teacher, accompanied Jim to Cherski as his translator and remained there, teaching school and learning from him for several years. Jim believed that living in Cherski amongst the Sakha, Evenk, Even and Chuckchi people, was a fulfillment of the Athabaskan elder's prophesy. There is virtually no place on earth where people live farther north than Cherski. Living and working there to help deal with problems related to alcohol, Jim felt he was igniting a small match that would become a burning torch. He believed that torch would one day come back across the land bridge and bring the light from the North back to Alaska.

After Jim's death, wanting to continue the work he had begun and honor his memory, I invited Tatyana Martynova to visit me in Juneau. I first met Tonya when I went to Yakutia in 1997 at Jim's urging to take part in a healthy lifestyles conference he and Tonya spearheaded at the small college there. Tonya and I became instant soul sisters and friends. We worked together for many years on numerous health, education and economic development exchanges between Alaska and the Sakha Republic. After Jim's death, we both felt lost as to how to continue his work and how to make it our own. Face-to-face discussions seemed like a good idea. It was during those discussions, that the idea for the Women's Voices Project took shape.

Tonya would travel with me from the North to the South along the "good red road" and interview grandmothers in Russia, Alaska and the United States. We would do it alone, funded only by our sacrifices and the assistance of the Creator.

We would ask the grandmothers to share their wisdom with the world. We would put our lives in God's hands and find people along the way from all walks of life – the only common denominator among the people we would interview was that they would all be mothers and grandmothers. And we would ask each one to share with us what she had learned along her life's journey. If we profited from our efforts, we would use a portion of the profits to create a Women's Center in Yakutsk dedicated to helping women, mothers, and handicapped children, and dedicated to changing lives.

The Other Travelers

I first met Nadia Noeva when she served as a translator at a healthy lifestyles conference held outside Yakutsk in 2002. At that conference, she shared with me that one of her dreams was to become a filmmaker, someone who could capture the beauty and majesty of her traditional Sakha culture before it was gone. Her sincerity to fulfill that dream was infectious.

Our final traveler, Cheryl Eldemar, a Tlingit woman from Juneau, had been invited by Jim years before to become part his work in Russia. Though she did not, Cheryl's path and mine continued to cross for many years. When the idea of the Women's Voices Project was born, Cheryl agreed to come along on the journey.

The Plan to Fly

As with many significant events in people's lives, the picture of how the Women's Voices Project would evolve was painted only in broad brush strokes. The plan was to not have a plan. Nadia and Tonya would meet me in Seattle with tickets paid for from the sale of my home. Together we would find a Best Buy, purchase needed camera equipment, and start driving south. Thanks to the hospitality of a good friend, I had a place to stay in the Seattle area after my voyage on the Alaska Marine Highway came to an end. My friend's home became a sanctuary while I waited for Tonya and Nadia to arrive. Cheryl would join me later, and become my traveling companion after the other women returned to Yakutsk to resume their lives. As the writer and producer, I was responsible for editing the interviews and somehow, I would write the book, find a filmmaker and publisher, and the rest would be history. At the start, that was all I could see. That, and a dream assuring me that when I flew off the second platform and didn't go back to my safe lodge, somehow I would fly.

Essential Questions

There were nine essential questions we set out to find answers to along the journey. We asked the women to share their most difficult experience in life and what gave them the strength to overcome it. We wanted to know who and what the women had drawn on for support during difficult times. We asked what in life had brought them the most joy. What was their proudest moment, accomplishment or experience? And we wanted to know if there was anything these grandmothers thought was important when they were young that they later realized wasn't meaningful or important. We asked if there were any "lies" they had believed to be true about themselves or about the world that they now knew had never been true. We wanted to know their greatest regrets, their biggest mistakes. And we wanted to know the one most important piece of advice they could give their daughters and granddaughters. Lastly, we asked the grandmothers if there was anything from their culture or their upbringing they thought was important to share and preserve.

The Women, The Grandmothers

The women we interviewed ranged from age 44 to 102. They were black, white, brown, yellow and every mix between. They were Yurok, Navajo, Tlingit, Irish, Russian, English, Iranian, Armenian, South African, Chinese, Chumash and more. They were Christians, Jews, Baha'is, Muslims, agnostics, and those who practiced their Native ways. They lived in a San Francisco mansion, a Sausalito houseboat, a trailer in Yuma, a homeless shelter in Portland, a retirement community in Tempe, a cabin in Alaska, and state housing in Yakutsk. They lived in Siberian villages, Alaskan towns, cities and suburbs across the Lower 48. They lived on mountains, tundra, plains, mesas, deserts and ocean sides. They voted for Herbert Hoover, Franklin D. Roosevelt, Ronald Regan, George Bush and Barak Obama. One escaped religious persecution by leading her children across the mountains from Iran to Pakistan and into freedom. One escaped sexual slavery and physical mutilation. They were attorney generals, recovering addicts, nurses, teachers, homemakers, authors, and waitresses. They were married for 65 years, divorced after 60 years, widowed, rich, poor, abused, abandoned, honored, and forgotten. We met them all along our journey and they welcomed us into their lives. We met them in parking lots, on their streets, in coffee houses and on the beach. We approached them as strangers and left as friends. They shared their experience, strength, hopes and dreams, freely and for the asking. Their wisdom changed us forever. We welcome you to hear the Women's Voices and learn the wisdom of the grandmothers.

Tatyana Martynova: Respect and Forgiveness

Tatyana (Tonya) Martynova was born in a village in the Sakha Republic (Yakutia). She is one of seven children, six girls and one boy. She has one son, Vladimir, and one grandson. Tonya worked closely with Tlingit elder Jim Walton in Cherski, where she taught at a college and was the organizer of several international gatherings with Jim to address the alcohol problem in the Sakha Republic. She also helped start The Tundra Women's Center in Cherski, the first women's shelter in the Russian Far East. Tonya's interview started out to help us test the camera, but soon took on a life of its own.

"My parents were very hard working," Tonya said. "I didn't know my father well growing up. He was always working. Before he died he told me stories of his childhood and his life. He died two years ago, but I still have the feeling of not enough time with my father. I am still grieving and it is still hard for me to talk about him. I love him very much and I miss him."

"When something bad happens in my life he always comes to my dreams – like he is trying to prevent me from something bad happening. People say I have a spiritual connection with him. In these dreams he is very sad. When I wake up from these dreams, I always start to cry. I just feel sorry that I didn't spend enough time with him when he was alive."

Tonya said that in many ways she and her father shared similar personalities. "He never showed his feelings even if he was sad. Even before dying he never showed that he was suffering. He broke a leg and he was in the bed for one month or more. My sisters refused to take care of him because they couldn't forgive his attitude when we were growing up. I tried to explain to them, 'This is our father. Let's forgive. Let's take care of him,' but they refused to come and visit him."

"At the last moments in his life I took him to my mom's house and when my sisters came to mom's house I told them, 'He is dying. Before it is too late you should come and see him.' But in the end he didn't recognize them. After he died my sisters cried and said, 'You did the right thing to bring him to mom's house and give us a chance to see him.' But for some of my sisters it was too late."

"I started to think that my dad was working all his life to support this big family, and at the end of his life there was just one daughter taking care of him. It's not fair. For what had he lived his life? He was working hard."

Tonya said understanding her father's childhood helped her to forgive. "He was sometimes violent, but his childhood was after the revolution. My grandma, when she give birth to my father, she told my grandpa that my father was going to die because the Red Army was coming and they were going to come and kill everyone anyway. She told him, 'Take this baby and just throw him to the snow. He will die anyway.' But my grandfather took the baby and put him in with the cows. It was warm and he survived because he hid him with the cows. When he was saying all this, I had to understand his behavior because there was no love from his mother right when he come to this world. That is why it started that he was sometimes violent and angry. But I forgive him because I understood."

Tonya said that when she faces challenges and difficulties in her life she actually gets stronger and more focused. "I concentrate and become stronger to do what I have to. I can't go and cry. It's not my style. I do what I have to do and just go."

"Sakha women, we don't cry on someone's shoulder. It's not our style to share with each other even if we have problems. We try to keep silent."

But the Sakha tradition of keeping silent, Tonya said, should perhaps change. "Maybe it's not good. I think it's time to change. It's too hard to keep to yourself. You should share with other women - it will be easier to live."

"Maybe it's an old model. Some people say it's because of our severe climate and that we live isolated from each other - that's why it's like that. It forms our national character. I read a book that before the October Revolution, Sakha women committed suicide because they had no help and they had a very bad position in the family. But now it's a different picture."

Although Tonya has numerous personal and professional accomplishments, as she has gotten older, her own perceptions of what is important in life have changed and her focus now is on her family. "Before something I was proud of was my graduation from my first university. I graduated with a red diploma and at that time it was very rare for women. Or I would have said the conferences I helped put on in Cherski or Yakutsk were something to be proud of. But now I think that's not so important. Now I think the most important thing was that I forgave my father and I have a spiritual connection with him. Before, I just tried to avoid him because it was very hard for me. But now that I found the strength to overcome my feelings and just forgive him and take care of him - he died in my hands - for me, I think that is the most important."

As for advice for young women, Tonya said that respect is the most important. "First of all always respect people, because if you lose that there is no future. We should keep our links between family members because if someone his hurting or suffering in a family, it will go from generation to generation. We have to try and solve our family problems first so that we can help future generations have a more happy life."

She also said it's important to try to see things from other people's perspective. "I always try to understand. If something is wrong, I try to look on the other side – to look more broadly and to try to think from a different position. I think it's easier in life if you try to be in someone else's shoes."

Elizaveta Aleksandrovna Ivanova: Light from the North

Elizaveta Aleksandrovna Ivanova was born in the Suntarksiy Region of the Sakha Republic (Yakutia). She is the mother of three daughters and the proud grandmother of one granddaughter. Elizaveta is the mother of Nadia Noeva, the Women's Voices Project camera woman, translator and fellow traveler on the journey.

Elizaveta Aleksandrovna Ivanova was born in 1934 in the rural Suntarksiy region of Russia's Sakha Republic (Yakutia). She is the mother of three daughters, Nadia, an English teacher, translator and filmmaker, Sahaiya, a manager, and Lena, a violinist. Her son-in-law is a businessman and her four-year-old granddaughter, Elena, is the light of her life.

As a child, Elizaveta grew up as an orphan. "As an orphan I realized very well that I was all alone with no mother or father. I always had this idea in my mind and I had to deal with other people from this point of view most of the time as a child," she said.

"I used to live with different families and though sometimes they would be cruel to me and punish me, I never argued with them and I never had my own opinion what-so-ever, because I knew that I had no right to argue with them. If I had argued with them I could have become a homeless person."

Elizaveta said it was nature that gave her strength to overcome her difficulties as a child. "I would draw support from nature, from the trees, from the valleys. I would always go out and sing some songs and I think nature became like my mother and my father at that time. I would go there and express my joy and happiness, my grief and sorrow. Nature was something I enjoyed the most at that time in my life."

"When my dad was dying he said to me that I should become an educated person," she said. "Those were his last words and he would always repeat them again and again. All my life I tried and I did my best to become educated."

"When I finished school I went to the collective farm to work as a milkmaid and I did a lot of different work there. I worked for five years, saved some money and decided to become a student. I entered the University and chose to become a veterinarian."

Elizaveta said she was a good student. "I studied very well, finished the University and did become a vet. My professors liked me very much and one of them particularly supported me in those years. He would help prepare me for my exams and he was a great support."

As a veterinary student she was given the task of doing scientific research, but unfortunately wasn't able to finish the research at the time. Later in life she decided to enter the University again and get a second diploma. "That is why I went back and studied biology; to accomplish the task that I was given by the other faculty," she said. Doing so eliminated a regret she had carried.

"I chose to get married and my greatest dream was to have children," she said. "I am very proud that I had children. I wanted them to become good people and to accomplish their own life dreams; to be successful in their own lives."

Although Elizaveta was very happy to graduate from the university, she said her happiest moment in life was when she became a grandmother. "When my daughter was giving birth, I just knew it was happening. When I became a grandmother, I felt in a different way. I feel the sun is different and the world is different. I have something new in my life. It was the greatest moment."

One of the things that changed in her life as she has become older, Elizaveta said, is her attitude toward what love is. "When you are young, you believe in love. You think that love is something and when you fall in love with someone that person becomes an ideal to you. You think about that person all the time. But as time passes it is interesting to note that attitude toward love changes a lot. It is totally different from what I thought when I was young to what I think as an old person."

As for advice for young women, Elizaveta stressed the importance of couples being supportive to each other. "They should be peaceful and have a wonderful attitude toward their families, so they can build their own families and have their own children. I just want them to be happy."

Although she is happy to have accomplished her personal and professional goals in life – including purchasing her own home, something still relatively rare in the Sakha Republic - Elizaveta said her life's greatest accomplishment is her three daughters and granddaughter. "That is my biggest joy."

The Sun is Different, The World is Different

"When I became a grandmother, I felt a different way. I feel that the sun is different and the world is different. I have something new in my life. It was the greatest moment."

—Elizaveta Aleksandrovna Ivanova

Vera Lee Justice Earl: A Life of Beauty

Vera Lee Justice Earl grew up in the tiny rural town of Dacula, Georgia, the daughter of Herman and Jessie Justice. She is the mother of three children, the grandmother of eight and a longtime beautician in Juneau, Alaska. Vera's kindness, generosity of spirit, and personal support made her a perfect candidate for the Women's Voices Project.

Vera Lee Justice Earl grew up in the tiny rural town of Dacula, Georgia, one of five children of Herman and Jessie Justice. Ducula, according to Vera, is somewhere between Atlanta and Athens, Georgia - the kind of town that "if you blinked, you would miss it." Her first house was four rooms with no running water or indoor plumbing. "My siblings and I slept in the same bedroom," she said. "We didn't know any different, we were young and we were happy."It wasn't until she was six, when her grandfather helped find a new house for the family, that Vera experienced running water and a bathroom for the first time. "It was a big farmhouse with lots of outdoor buildings and barns. My dad tore down all the buildings and we all pitched in and planted Bermuda grass in rows all through the huge yard. There were big oak trees and one huge Magnolia, with ivy running on the trees in the old Southern style."

Vera went to elementary and high school in Dacula, in a school system that wasn't integrated until the year after she graduated.

"I was 19 years old when I married for the first time. I married my high school sweetheart. My husband knew he was going to get drafted to go to Vietnam, so he joined the Air Force. We got married right before he went in to basic training. He got sent to Michigan and I went with him."

Vera had her first child at age 20. "Our first year of marriage was in Michigan, and it was probably good for me. I was a hometown girl who had never been anywhere. It really was the best thing that ever happened, because I got out of that little town and saw life is a little different in other places. I made a lot of friends and we all had babies together."

But Vera said her first husband was very domineering. "He didn't want me to go outside the house without him. He was jealous, domineering and possessive. He was also an introvert and didn't want friends or family over. Things started changing for me after our second child. I felt like I was having to sneak to have a little fun or go to talk with a friend. We went back to Georgia and that's when I really started to get discontent."

"I lived in a mobile home in my parents' backyard when my husband went to Thailand during the war. My mother-in-law tried to plan my day. When my husband and I were separated for a year, that's when I started to think about things."

Vera said she was raised in the Baptist Church where the husband in the head of the household. "I was raised to be a good girl, to listen to my husband. I enjoyed being a mother and was very conscious of the children's health and school. We were very active in our church; we went every Sunday."

After her last child was born Vera went back to work in a beauty salon. "I had worked for my aunt while I was in high school. She was a hairstylist and I got to apprentice with her. Once I went back to work, looking back on it, I think that was when I started planning a divorce. I started saving cash."

"I was terrified. What was I going to do out there on my own? I had to make a living. My son was six and my oldest was 10. I started working full time and I went to school for a year to get my license."

"We had built a beautiful, three story house. My husband was an electrician. His father was an electrician too. We borrowed $29,000 and built this fabulous, three story house with four bedrooms and three baths. My husband's family gave us the property right next door to their place, by a big creek. It had a big bridge and a big beautiful yard. I had what most people would have looked at on the outside as a wonderful marriage. But on the inside, I was pretty miserable. I couldn't go anywhere or do anything. I felt really stifled. I had been in that house for three years and I decided that we just weren't meant for each other. I grew up and he stayed the same."

"I went to him one day and said, 'I want a divorce.' Life is too short and I want to move on.' He had not a clue. He was livid."

Vera said her husband wanted to start over and perhaps move away from living near his domineering parents. "I thought about it but I realized I didn't love him anymore.

My parents were devastated. They thought it was me. You wouldn't believe the things they said. I kept to myself for a long time. But I felt really comfortable when I realized I could take care of myself."

Vera said marrying so young had left her feeling she had missed out on fun. "I started driving to another town on the weekends, just to go out and have fun. I did that for two years, and then I met my current husband, Richard, through my best friends. The first time I met him I thought, 'Oh no, he has too much hair! He was riding a motorcycle and looked all ragged out. I was looking for a guy in a three piece suit!"

"We met again about a year later. He was looking for a date to go to a friend's wedding. When he asked me out he said, 'I'll wear a three piece suit! And by the way, I shaved!' We've been together for the last 28 years."

Vera said that when she thinks about the lessons she has learned in life, she realizes that a person can't be too quick to make decisions. "You have to think things through. I wanted to marry to get out of the house when I was young. I knew I couldn't afford a college education, so getting married was my ticket out. But I realized that's not the answer. You have to plan your life. You have to have some sort of a plan and not just jump for one thing or the other."

"Having a career has kept me going. I sometimes see 10 people in a day. I get to socialize. My clients tell me their innermost secrets. Each one of my clients is my friend. I really enjoy that."

Vera said girlfriends are important, too. "Girls need each other. Girls need to have fun together. We have fun with our husbands, but with our girlfriends it's a whole different ball game."

"My children are a wonderful part of my life. Staying good friends with your children is important too. If I had any advice to give young women it would be to take your time. Life is good. Don't sweat the little things. Wait things out and don't jump the gun. You have your whole life ahead of you."

"Another thing I have learned is that finances have a place in happiness, but you really don't have to have a lot of things. I don't have to have brand name things or a big house anymore to be happy. I really think getting in debt and overextending yourself is a big mistake. Being in debt is very stressful and it can disrupt a happy marriage."

" I realized that life is full of mystery. And the world is so full of beauty. Don't miss the beauty."

Beauty

*"I realized that life is full of mystery.
And the world is so full of beauty.
Don't miss the beauty."*

—Vera Lee Justice Earl

Jeannette Marie Camino Turton: Family, Faith and Fun

I met Jeannette Turton, of Indiana, Pennsylvania, when she was sitting with her husband on the maroon benches in the cafeteria of the M/V Malispina, somewhere between Auke Bay and British Columbia. The quiet hum of the ship's engine, the blue-grey waters of the Inside Passage, and the snow-capped mountain peaks were the scene for this mother of four and grandmother of seven's Elder Hostel Alaska adventure and the backdrop for our Women's Voices interview.

Jeannette Marie Camino Turton grew up in Cleveland, Ohio, the daughter of Italian immigrants to the United States. A first generation American, all four of her grandparents lived in the village of Ururi, Italy. She described her early life as not unlike many others of her generation: her father worked for Carlings Brewery in Cleveland, Ohio until it closed and her grandparents cared for her and her brother while her mother worked as a "Rosie the Riveter" during World War II. She grew up, went to Notre Dame College, a women's school in South Euclid, Ohio became a history teacher, got married and started her family right away.

"With the birth of my twins, I managed to have four babies in 27 months. We lived hand to mouth while my husband attended graduate school. He had a grant from the National Institute for Health of $5,600 a year. Thank God the All Star Dairy made home deliveries! At the end of the month we'd have very little left and they would deliver milk and eggs and cheese. I used to buy 220 jars of baby food a month for the twins!"

"I learned to sew just so I could dress the kids. I made everything they wore. My husband Larry had to wear white shirts at the clinic and when his collars wore out, I would take the shirt material to make tops for the girls that I would decorate with appliqués."

Jeannette said her early years of marriage were spent thousands of miles from family, without any help. "I remember one day the lady next door came to help me fold diapers and I was so thankful. Those were the hardest years. I remember when my husband was getting his Ph.D., my cousin Joe sent $50 for Christmas to buy the kids some things. He told us to save $25 to out to dinner and we did! It was amazing!"

"When my husband finished school we moved to Kansas City and rented a little bungalow with an upstairs. I remember there were no heating vents in the upstairs and I called the City of Kansas City to complain. I was quite perturbed!"

Jeannette said that one hardest times she remembers was when she spent time in the hospital after the birth of her twins. "Relatives took care of the kids. I had just had the twins a month before and I passed out from the pain. I had to go back to the hospital for gallbladder surgery. The doctor wouldn't let me go home to take care of the babies. My mother took my son and my mother-in-law took the twins. It was a very hard time."

For Jeannette, her mother and mother-in-law provided inspiration and strength for overcoming life's difficulties. "My mother was a phenomenal woman and a great inspiration. My mother-in-law had 10 kids. They were both very strong women and I tried to imitate them."

When she went to college, Jeannette said both of her grandmothers had a fit. "But my father told them that I would be a better mother for it. And I firmly believe that. The nuns used to say, 'Educate a man and you educate a person. Educate a woman and you educate a family.' My father understood that."

As for her husband, Jeannete described him as "a hell of a guy."

"He never shirked his fatherly duty. He took charge of the kids when I needed him and I never had the feeling that I was raising the kids alone. Larry and I are probably each other's best friends. That's the most important thing in marriage. We haven't gotten tired of each other yet! We are founding members of the Indiana Ballroom Dance Club. When my girls got engaged we decided we needed to dance, so we took ballroom dance and we've been dancing ever since."

Jeannette said that along with her family, she drew strength in her life from her church. "I love going to church. I'm a people person, and I really like the people. We have gone to the same church for almost 30 years. We have a core group of friends that we spend a lot of time talking about faith. All of us have the same problems, the same experiences."

Jeannette's greatest source of pride is her children. "We got all four kids through college. We have a daughter who is learning disabled and had to work harder as a result of it, but she earned a BA in history, an MA in archival history and a Master's degree in library sciences. I am so proud of all of my children! It's because of them that I decided to go back to school myself and earn my Master's degree in Early Childhood Education."

Yet despite that pride, Jeannette's cites something different as her life's greatest accomplishment. "I hope it's not willingly hurting anyone."

"I've tried really hard to be a good teacher, mother and grandmother. If I have any advice to give to the next generation, it would be to be patient. Don't be afraid to keep on learning. Don't be afraid to admit mistakes. Don't forget to vote. Pay your bills on time and learn the perils of debt. Love each other. And have fun!"

Hope and Unity

"I had a real sense of wanting to reassure people that there was hope, that there was a reason for the things that have happened to us, that we could overcome the difficulties we had in common. And part of it was to begin to unite as a family again and gradually to take that to the larger levels where we would unite as tribal people and begin to unite as nations. And of course that is taking us to the level of the world, where the world has to look at the things that divided us. And that we individually have a choice that we can make that can set a whole change in motion."

—Lauretta Walton King

Lauretta Walton King: A Life of Service, a Life of Faith

Although the plan for the Women's Voices journey was to meet the women we interviewed along the way, there were a few women I knew I wanted to visit. One of those women was Jim Walton's cousin, Lauretta Walton King, a woman he highly admired for her faith and her service. Tonya and Nadia had just arrived in Seattle from Yakutsk, and we decided to travel up the scenic Olympic Peninsula to see Lauretta at her home in Bremerton, Washington.

Lauretta Walton King was born and raised in Sitka, a small Alaskan town where snow capped mountains rise majestically out of the ocean. The towering green Sitka Spruce and Hemlock contrast against the blue and grey skies and set a grand background for the bald eagles that fly overhead in great circles. Sitka was the original Russian capital of Alaska. As a young girl, Lauretta remembered hearing stories from her uncles and grandparents of the way it used to be before contact with the west. Her father, William Rudolph Walton, was Tlingit and her mother Laura Newgent Walton was half Russian and half Tlingit.

"When I look back at my life it always amazes me just how fortunate I was, how guided and protected my life seemed to be."

Her upbringing included both learning traditional Tlingit ways and becoming educated in the modern world. For Lauretta, that upbringing included a life committed to and connected to the Creator.

"The most important aspect of my life on this earth is that there is a spiritual life. Beyond the things that happen, we need to be in touch with the spiritual world, that side that makes us an even better human being. That would be the prime, important thing that I would hope to instill in the next generation."

"I remember one winter when it was already snowing and it was just before it got really not wise to travel. We were going out to one of the small villages by airplane along the river system and were planning on stopping in a particular village before it got dark, which at that time of year is quite early in Alaska."

"But we ran into a snow storm. It was a dense enough storm that we had to travel just above the height of the trees at the edge of the riverbank. And of course the river was frozen, and it was all white and the trees were all white from the previous snow and the current snow. We knew we had about 45 minutes to go to the next village, because there just weren't villages all along the edge of the river."

"I think it was a time that really caused me to rely on the thing that has sustained me all my life. And of course that was a sense of prayer: prayer to the Creator, prayer to the Almighty, prayer to those ancestors that seemed to have guided me through my life."

"It was dusk and it was really getting to a serious situation about the time that we landed. We ended up in a village that we hadn't planned to land in. It was one that came up a little bit earlier and it turned out that the people there were so warm, so welcoming. It just made it really a special experience."

"As a young child my mother had such an appreciation of the Creator, attached with a belief in God and a belief in a way of life that affected her. And she passed that on to me in a number of different ways including saying a prayer at night before we went to sleep and seeing that I was able to get a religious education in the community I grew up in. It really helped to instill in me an appreciation for the fact that there is a Higher Power, there is somebody that is guiding our lives, that there is a purpose to life. And that has carried me through the years and I think that it had such a profound effect on the things I have been able to do. If I have been able to accomplish anything, undoubtedly it had an effect on that."

King's accomplishments are many. She was the wife of the late Lynn King of Sitka, and the mother of three sons, William, Michael and Steven King, and one daughter, Laurie King. She is also the proud grandmother of four grandchildren.

When asked her proudest moments in life, she said it would be hard to single out one. "When I was growing up the fact that I was able to excel in school and was able to speak for the class in an honorary way. That was a proud moment. And when my husband and I married and we were able to look forward to a life together; that was a proud moment," she said.

"Early in our marriage I became a member of the Baha'i Faith, a follower of the teachings of Baha'u'llah, and that had a profound effect on my life. It was something that I felt I had been looking for and waiting for all of my life and in doing the things that I could to serve that Faith I was asked to do certain things throughout the years and each of them had a degree of pride to them."

"The one moment that had the highest, such a feeling of awe, was that I would be considered to be among those to work in Israel in really a special office, with a special group of people that were involved with teaching and helping to educate the friends in a spiritual path; and that took us around the world." Lauretta served for many years as a member of the International Teaching Center for the Baha'i World Faith in Haifa, Israel.

"Without a doubt, that was a very proud moment to be able to do that. Here was a person who had grown up in a very small community in Alaska, and who had been able to undertake some travel, but to be asked to serve in a capacity like that was extremely humbling and extremely fulfilling."

Lauretta's service to her Faith took her around the world and enabled her to share her culture with indigenous people from Barrow, Alaska to Tierra del Fuego, Chile. "My life was affected very much by the teachings of the Baha'i Faith. They are teachings that help us to see that we have a role in serving mankind; to see that we have a role in bringing about the unity of peoples throughout the world."

"I can remember that at one time when I visited the Holy shrines and knelt in prayer that I wanted to offer whatever I could do to serve this Faith. And I felt very inadequate and very limited in what I could do. But I just really wanted to do that. And it seems that really it opened up a whole new width to the path and a whole new depth to the path, and I found myself being asked to serve in different capacities."

"I especially enjoyed the travel to meet indigenous people and to share some of the things from the cultures that had talked about a historical point in time when people began to travel again and began to come together. First my travel was within Alaska, and then it extended to Canada. Then later I was invited to travel throughout the Americas. At one point I found myself in Barrow, Alaska on the last day when the sun came up, so it was in mid-November. And then a month later I was in Tierra del Fuego in the southern tip of Chile and being able to go meet people and talk with them and to try to give them that sense of hope and the fact that there were things that they had been waiting for in their prophesies and the stories that the medicine men told them to expect were happening. And that this was the time when we were to come together and it was an extremely exciting thing."

"I had a real sense of wanting to reassure people that there was hope, that there was a reason for the things that have happened to us, that we could overcome the difficulties we had in common. And part of it was to begin to unite as a family again and gradually to take that to the larger levels where we would unite as tribal people and begin to unite as nations. And of course that is taking us to the level of the world, where the world has to look at the things that divided us. And that we individually have a choice that we can make that can set a whole change in motion."

When asked if there was something from her upbringing or culture that she wanted to pass on to the next generations, Lauretta said it would certainly be what her mother passed on to her.

"Along with the spiritual life, the second would be to try and do the best that each person could in receiving an education. And that education could be in different ways, not all of it had to be scholastic where everyone went to get their degree. But if they didn't follow that route, which was an honorable one certainly to do, but to have some training in some field so that they would be able to work to raise their families. That was my heart's desire, and hopefully to a limited degree, I have been able to do that."

My Friendship Community

"What gave me the strength to overcome all life's hardships were my friends, my friendship community ... The biggest thing that came from that experience wasn't getting over the alcohol and drugs; but it was the understanding that at a time of crisis, if you can get together with people who have the same concerns and the same values, you can make a difference."

—Ann Matranga

Larissa Williams: Reaching For The Helping Hand

We met Larissa Williams at the Sisters of the Road Café located in the Old Town/Chinatown neighborhood in Portland, Oregon. The community is home to hundreds of low income and homeless residents, many of whom are customers of Sisters. According to the Sisters literature, "when the old café opened in 1979, the neighborhood marked our doorstep with an old hobo symbol, a circle containing three X's, meaning good food and hospitality can be found inside." Larissa came to Sisters for a hot meal and a helping hand. We came to Sisters looking for its founder, but instead found inspiration in Larissa's journey.

Larissa Williams hit rock bottom living on the streets of Portland, addicted to alcohol and drugs. She had made the decision to get off the streets only two weeks before. "I get my mail here, take a shower here, and eat here," she said, referring to the Sisters of the Road cafe. "They really help a lot of people on the streets. I just made the decision that I didn't want to live on the streets anymore. I decided to get help."

"I was living up under the bridge on 4th Street. I slept on the concrete. (Name deleted) had molested my child and that's what first put me on the streets. Then I had breast cancer and had a mastectomy and I was living on drugs and just didn't care. I was taking Vicodin and Demerol, and I just started taking more and more. I couldn't stop taking the pills, getting high and smoking crack."

"I lived like that for two and a half years, walking around, sitting on a bench on the street. But my sister Kendra came down and found me on the streets and reached out a hand. She told me, 'I care.' I realized that I was tired of the way I was living and decided I really did want to live again. I realized that I need to live for myself and for my kids. Now, I am in the treatment center and coming here to get help. I want to live. On my own, my brain is trained to think ugly stuff. Now I know I have to have a Higher Power to get through the day. I think I can make it if I just grab on."

*** To find out more about how to donate to Sisters of The Road go to www.sistersoftheroad.org*

Sonia Lee Chou: Respect for Your Culture, Respect for Yourself, Respect for Others

Sonia Lee Chou first came to the United States from Taiwan, China on a school holiday. The daughter of Ching Hui Lee and Funguh Chang Lee, and the mother of Delia Chou, Sonia first moved to San Luis Obisbo, California. She later moved with her husband to run a motel in Cresent City, a small town along California's northern coast nestled amidst the towering, giant Redwood forest, where we met her.

"My husband loves the trees here, and in five minutes we can get everywhere in town. It's a small town so we know everyone," Sonia said.

Knowing people is important to Sonia now.

"When I finished college in Taiwan, my sister was in Japan. First, when I went to Japan, there were so many things to learn. Then when I came to the United States and it was very difficult because there was no family."

For Sonia, learning the language of her adopted country presented a huge challenge. "When I went to Japan, I had to learn Japanese and when I came to the United States, I had to change from Japanese to English. If you don't know the language well, it is hard to communicate deeply. I would really encourage people who want to go to another country to learn the language and don't stay with your people. Go to a small town and get to know the people and to know their lives. Otherwise I would say it is very hard."

"This is a very lovely country. People are very patient and they have good hearts. I had a restaurant for 10 years; and my guests were my teachers. They don't look down on you. In the United States people allow you to do mistakes."

"I always encourage people about Americans. If you have dreams in this country, your dreams will come true. People will help you out for no reason, no payback. People are just willing to help you out."

Despite her love for her new homeland, Sonia is proudest of being Chinese. "I think being Chinese is being proud too. It's not about the lifestyle; it is about the rich culture. There are some virtues inside of us already. You respect your parents, not just by education or by tradition. It is inside of us. If you follow your conscience then you go to any country and you can be yourself. I am so proud that I have that within me."

As Sonia has grown older, she realized that the focus she put on acquiring material things when she was younger was really not important.

"When I was young I thought that being rich was the important thing, but now I think that it's not the only thing. Before I would think that with money or material things, you show off yourself. But now I don't care about how people think. If you are comfortable and you are healthy that's important. When I saw my parents in the hospital, I realized that material things cannot buy peace. People should focus on more spiritual things - on conservation, not on collection."

"I used to have a tough life too. I liked to challenge myself. I came to the U.S. and I had friends who were very patient, and we always laughed at them. We would think, 'Why are you so stupid, to care about other people?' But then I realized that if people can use them as a model and care about other people, the world will become peace. And that is when I started to change myself."

"Now everyone walking in the store is my brother and sister. It doesn't matter that the language or the color of skin might be different, but they all come from their parents. The spirit comes from the same area."

"I always tell my daughter that it is very important to study because to study is one part that brings knowledge. But the most important thing is virtue. If you see moms outside on the street, treat everyone like your mom. If you see grandparents, see your own grandparents. If you see someone your age, see your brother and sister. If you see someone younger, you are always taking care of them like a brother and sister. It is important to have this mindset. You need other people wherever you go. You will have peace if you treat people like that."

For Sonia, there is one thing she has learned in her new culture that she thinks is very important to share with other women.

"I think that the women are very different in my culture and this culture. In my culture, we depend on the men. In this culture, women should challenge themselves. You don't have to depend on someone else. Here if you depend on the men, you can also stand up yourself. You can drive yourself. You can go anywhere yourself.... Get back your life for yourself, not for someone else. Be independent. A husband

and wife have to be like yin and yang, but you have to be able to survive if you are alone."

"When I first came here when it was getting dark I would be lonely, feeling like I was floating without safety and security. Now I tell any guests that come to this place, you have safety and security. I always try to make them feel they know someone here and they don't have to worry."

"I think that every moment of life is very important; the moment of the truth. … Every moment is very important to everyone. I think that time runs out so fast and people have to try to enjoy every moment. Do not hurt someone else, but to try to enjoy every moment. Everyone is special. Everyone is a gift from God."

Love Each Other and Have Fun

"If I have any advice to give to the next generation, it would be to be patient. Don't be afraid to keep on learning. Don't be afraid to admit mistakes. Don't forget to vote. Pay your bills on time and learn the perils of debt. Love each other. And have fun!"

—Jeannette Turton

Amanda Simms Donahue: Preserving the Yurok Ways

Amanda Simms Donahue works as a receptionist for the Yurok Tribe on the reservation outside of Klamath, California. Her back yard is the Redwood forest, the Klamath River runs through her land, and growing things on the land provides her healing. We met Amanda when we decided to try to find the tribal headquarters for the people indigenous to the magnificent Redwood forest.

"As a child I remember everything being a lot simpler than it is now. I remember thinking that my little part of the world was really the only one that existed. My father was quite a bit older than my mother. He was almost 30 years older than her. His birthday was 1892. So I grew up with an older father that was more like a great grandfather than a father. But he was dedicated and loving and he taught me a lot about growing vegetables. That was what we did; we grew a lot of vegetables."

"I inherited the land from him that was passed down from his grandfather and grandmother, and my goal is to start a vegetable garden there that can be a community garden for the people."

"Growing up it was a lot different than it is now. I felt more segregated. Even though we didn't have an established Yurok tribe like we do now. We didn't have anything like it is now, I always knew that I was Yurok. We have gone by different names but I always chose Yurok for many reasons."

"When I started school, it was a whole different program for me. I discovered I was a lot different from the kids that were in my classroom. I felt kind of alienated. Even though I didn't speak fluent Yurok, my dad did. And I encountered a whole lot of feelings that I never experienced before. I didn't get along very good with the Caucasians or white people that were in the schools. I didn't agree with their type o f discipline or education. I was kind of a rebellious child. But it was a lot simpler and a lot of aspects of our culture weren't being practiced then. It was like in the dark ages of our culture. But for some reason – I guess it was my father – I felt really warm and kind of enclosed in my culture even though we weren't really practicing it. A lot of dances were brought back in the '70s and now we are practicing a lot more dances in my culture than we did as a child, but still in my mind and in my heart it will never be the same."

"We became a tribe in the late 1980s when they started organizing the federally recognized portion of the Yurok Tribe. It all started with a timber settlement. At one time we were part of the Hoopa Tribe. We didn't have any rights. With the formation of the tribe that changed. With all the meetings we began having I began realizing that we were a large numbered tribe. We voted on it and a lot of people decided they wanted to be members of the tribe. And it opened up a lot of things; to enhance our rivers; getting our homeland identified."

"We had the Jessie Short case, which paid off in 1995, when we received a $26,000 settlement. A handful of people started the case, and it went on for over 50 years. A lot of older people were angry about it. The money doesn't last long, and it doesn't go very far. But what we really had as a result of it was each other. I think sometimes we forget how lucky we are. We have come a long way."

"As I get older I have found that a lot of things I thought were important at one time have become even more important. Our culture has been dying away. With each elder that dies, a part of it dies. Even the language has lost something. I will hear someone talk the language and it doesn't sound anything like my dad. We have lost our spirituality, the purpose of our dances. A lot of that is because of drugs and alcohol. I still fight against that, not only as a personal demon, but as a whole tribe. I wish a lot of people of influence with the tribe would step up and abolish that in the tribe."

"I think the hardest thing in life was losing my dad in 1976. I tried to think of the things he instilled in me as a child and tried to fashion my life after that. Also, I lost my 14 month old grandson and I got through it drawing from the strength of knowing that he was with my father. Even thought he wasn't here with me, he is still here in spirit."

"My greatest joy has come from my children and knowing they are enrolled members of the Yurok tribe. Knowing the tribe's history and the accomplishments they have made over the years - that is a great accomplishment. I wish we had it when I was a child. Now they have a lot of opportunities."

"The most important piece of advice I'd like to give to our daughters is a piece of advice my dad gave me when I was nine. There was an argument going on and he said the most important thing is to treat people the way you want to be treated. You shouldn't fight. It went over my head, but as I got older, I saw a lot of disagreements and I think about that. Fighting isn't important. Sometimes you have to give a little

bit. You have to forgive and go on with what is important even though that is hard."

"My father taught me to love people. He was kind of a pillar in the community back then when I was little. People would come to him with their problems. Sometimes they wanted money and he would give what he could. He would always have words of advice. He was kind of shy and didn't like to talk to a lot of people, but he instilled in me to put family first. To love the family that you have and your friends, to respect the earth, to respect and be thankful for when you can go hunting or go fishing, to thank that deer or that fish for giving their life for your family. That has been lost. Now we go to supermarket all the time. That has been lost and I see all of that going downhill because we don't have respect."

"I feel really at peace when I can walk through the forest or along the river along the bank. It is something I have always done, something I have always had a lot of opportunity to do. All of the things in nature we can't explain, I think that God gave them to us for a reason. I think we have misused them - our trees, our fish. Our water is being polluted everywhere, not just here. A lot of it is going away. Our own river is going

away every year. I have always felt a connection with the plants. Watching them grow is something I have always enjoyed."

"God is my strength. I know that He does hear me. When I go out in nature, I feel more comfortable. I know that the Creator is there and he knows everything about our past, about what our cultures have gone through, about how hate has divided us. Deep down inside we are one universal soul; that is where I have found my strength."

"One of my goals is to start a place where someone who is in rehabilitation can come and garden. I think that is one of the most healing experiences you can have, working with the earth, being outdoors, watching something productive that you have done yourself. It is helpful. It is like therapy. That is one of my goals I would like to see that happen. I don't know how I can do it, but that is what I want to do."

"I think that women in my culture are the backbone - probably it is in most cultures, although we are a male oriented culture, if that makes sense. I think a lot of old traditions and laws and rules were made up to keep control of women, but really without us, they wouldn't have any control. That is the way it has been in my culture without realizing it. In my culture my mother was the end decision; it seemed like that."

"My advice to women today is to try to reach out and understand your children, even from the time they are little. I get a little teary eyed with this because sometimes I think I might have made some mistakes and my kids are still paying for it. I hate thinking like that, but try to understand. Don't be too quick to push them off - try and understand."

Virtues Inside Us

"I think being Chinese is being proud too. It's not about the lifestyle; it is about the rich culture. There are some virtues inside of us already. You respect your parents, not just by education or by tradition. It is inside of us. If you follow your conscience then you go to any country and you can be yourself. I am so proud that I have that within me."

—Sonia Lee Chou

nga: Drawing Strength from Community,
ho You Are

*Ann Matranga lives on a
houseboat at the foot of
the Golden Gate Bridge in
Sausalito, California. Born
in Long Island, N.Y., she is
the mother of two children,
Jonah and Kaela, and the
grandmother of Hanah,
Atlas and Anika. We met Ann
in the parking garage of
the theater in San Franciso
playing host to the Native
American Film Festival. She
gave us directions to the Festival and invited us to her houseboat in Sausalito the
next day, where we learned much more about how to get where we really want to go.*

Ann Matranga believes there are two kinds of difficult experiences. "One is the
short brief, scary one. The other is the long marathon-like one." When it comes
to the long ones, Ann cites her job as a single parent as her most difficult and most
rewarding experience.

"The hardest thing I ever did that I did well was being a single parent from the time
my children were age five and six on. I was a full-on single parent, plus making
the money. I was not the most mature young person in the world and made many
mistakes, but I gradually moved into the role of being a good parent. By the time
they were teenagers I was on the job. I was blessed with a community of friends and
we did things together. When I look back now and I watch my daughter with her
little children, I think, 'How in the world did I do it?' When I think of all the things I
have done in my life, I am sure there is nothing more important than raising my kids
and having things turn out OK."

Ann says it was her friends who gave her the strength to overcome all life's
hardships. "For me, I hate to say it - I never did like romance very well at all. I
have always messed up my romances, so far - but friendship I have always done
well. I have had long friendships. There is some song that says, 'I could never stand
without my friends.' That is how I raised my kids. That is how I did anything and
still to this day it is about community."

"When my son was in high school we had a lot of problems with drugs. And what we did was get together a group of the families the other young people who were also having trouble. We called ourselves a family group and what we did is we kind of circled the wagons around them. We would have a meal together once every month. That went on for two years and we would talk about our lives. We all brought food. We would sit in a circle and go around that circle every month. Each person, parents and children, we would talk about what happened in the month past and what we were going to do with our lives."

"We evolved a way of doing things. The children would always say they didn't want to come; but they would come and we would talk about what happened and what we were going to do. And by the time those young people graduated, everyone was clean and sober. Our conversations had evolved from talking about their problems to talking about our own lives. …So I think the biggest thing that came from that experience wasn't getting over the alcohol and drugs, but it was the understanding that at a time of crisis, if you can get together with people who have the same concerns and the same values, and you can make a difference."

"I adopted my daughter when she was four days old and when she was in her 20s she was having a really hard time. And she and I read a book that was called *The Primal Wound* about the problems of adopted children who had been separated from their birth mother even at birth. She was four days old and I nursed her. I was nursing my biological son at the time. He was only nine months old and I said, 'What difference does it make?' But it made a huge difference."

"Because of that, we set out to find her birth family and we did. We found her dad first. It was a research project because the records are sealed. But we got enough information to find him. By the way, it was thanks to the Baha'i Faith that we found him. It was one of the clues in the records. I knew he was a musician. They would give you an abstract that would give you only a few facts, but I am really good at talking so I could get the people in the agencies to give me a little bit more. I knew his name, his religion and that he was African American. So I wrote to the Baha'i web site and asked 'Does anyone remember this person?' They did and I got two emails in a day and was able to get in touch with him immediately."

"It took me another year to track down Kaela's birth mother. Her dad told me she died when she was only 33, so I thought maybe that's good enough. We found Phil so maybe we should just let it go. But Kaela said no, she wanted to find her birth mother's family. And I realized how important it was to her to know where she came from, who she looked like, what was the story, who wanted her, who didn't. Even though she was loved and our family was intact."

"We found her birth mother's mother, who we now think of as Grandma Jean. I thought I better call her first. Now, this was the white side of the family and I don't know what she knows. We knew that her daughter had died. It could be just grief provoking. But I called and her husband answered the phone. He is this fantastic old southerner named CB. They live in Florida, and he answered the phone."

"And I had made up this whole script of what I was going to say, because I was really nervous. And I said, 'I have some memorabilia from Denise, Kaela's birth mother, from Boston in 1970 and I want to give that to her grandmother, to Jean.' And immediately he was so warm and welcoming. 'She can't wait to talk to you, but she is out, I'll have her call you right away.'"

"He must have gone out to find her and she called up and I was still real hesitant. I was sort of beating around the bush. And finally Jean said to me, 'I think you better get to the point.' And I thought, OK. So I said, 'Well, I'm your daughter's birth child's adoptive mother.' And she started to cry. She was such an amazing woman, and she said, 'I don't want you to think that these are unhappy tears. This is the happiest day of my life.'"

"We couldn't have been more blessed, because these are people – every one of them, on both the mother's and the father's side - that we would have liked to meet for any reason, anywhere anytime. But we all met, we had a family reunion."

"Kaela is her birth father's only child. He was absolutely devastated when her birth mother passed away. They had been parted by then, but all his life he had worried about her. Likewise, her grandmother. She's the only grandchild and it's like, 'Kaela rules! Kaela's a princess,' which she had always believed herself to be. Now her dreams came true. They came to her wedding. Her birth father walked her down the aisle with me. It's just like a miracle. That's a happy story."

"I am very lucky. You know my dad said he was always lucky. My son is a rock musician by the way, and when my dad died on that very day Jonah wrote a song in his honor and it said, 'Oh I am so lucky, there is no one as lucky as me,' And he sang it and now several schools have taken it."

"My father was big on luck. I have this ring. He came from a very poor family. His father had emigrated from Poland. He was a Polish Jew. He came here leaving a wife and several children in Warsaw; they came later. And when they came my father was the first born in this country. His mother died when he was three months old and all the children went to orphanages. My father went to an Irish Catholic foster home and that is where he got to be Catholic. And when he was six his father took him back into his family. He had a very difficult time growing up, but when he was around 18 he went to a pawn shop and he saw a ring like this only it was silver and he got it. He thought it brought him luck."

"He went to New York and my father did have a very lucky life. When he met and married my mother, he had one made for her, only in gold. Now everyone has one. And it turns out – he didn't know it - but every symbol on this ring is a symbol of long life and good fortune! It's the crab, it's the eternal robe, it's the dolphin; it's just like a magic ring. Not that my life has been so easy, but I do feel very lucky!"

Ann was raised Catholic and did not know until she was adult that her grandparents actually were Jewish. "It was a big lie," she said. "And it was a very difficult and complicated matter to figure everything out once the truth was known. My parents had believed that was the best thing to do. I went to Catholic boarding school and I was almost 50 years old before I knew my father's family came from Poland. He told us they came from Alsace-Lorraine. It was kind of a clever choice, because who knows anyone from Alsace-Lorraine?"

"It had a huge effect on me. Some friends in San Francisco invited me when I was about 46 to go to temple with them. When I walked in, the first thing I noticed was I looked like the people there. Growing up, I so wanted to look like the other kids. I was aware somehow that I looked different. I tried really hard to adjust my appearance in every way that I could. I tried to be more athletic, like the kids I grew up with. When I went into that temple, I remember thinking, 'I look like these people!' It's kind of weird."

"My spiritual connection is ridiculously important. I believe it is pretty easy to keep in touch with people you love and talk to them when they die. It's almost like it's just past a veil somewhere. And I ask them to send me messages. The last year of my dad's life I had spent a great deal of time with him, because my mom was gone and he really needed my presence. After he died and I was pretty unhappy for a while. This little desk was in his room. I brought it back here with me and I had taken the contents of the desk out. One day I was feeling pretty low and I asked him as a spirit. I said, 'Dad, I need to know that you are OK and I need you to send me a message and it cannot be subtle. I need to know!' I had a box of stuff from this desk and maybe no more than 10 minutes later I picked it up and I flipped it into this desk and this card pad flipped over. I had asked him to tell me you're OK and I flipped it over, and this is what it said - "Ann, call her, I'm OK." I figured that was one of the best messages I ever got." Some of my friends don't believe this at all. I have friends who think when you're dead, you're gone and it's over. I say to them, 'If I die before you, I say keep a heads up. You'll be hearing from me!'"

Concrete Evidence of God

"What I would pass on to another woman is love yourself and find your own connection with God and define it for yourself. ... In this journey there are some questions I don't want to have to answer again. So let's put this one on the decided side. There is a God. How I may refer to Him, or Her, or It, or call Him, or Her or It, that may vary. But there is a Spirit, if it's nothing more definite than the love of the universe, the Divine. Whatever words may be appropriate, that I know. And in times when I feel most frustrated or confused, I can refresh myself with the recollection of my own specific experiences where the Divine was kind enough to give hard- headed me some concrete evidence of His or Her or Its existence."

—Amanda Metcalf

Amanda Metcalf: The Journey to Know and Love Yourself

Amanda Metcalf was born in Cairo, Illinois, the daughter of Charlotte Madeline Butler Grogan and Manuel Metcalf. She is the mother of one son, Matthew Metcalf Welch. She is an attorney, currently living outside of San Francisco. We first met Amanda at the Native American Film Festival and were able to catch up with her at her home prior to our return north.

For Amanda Metcalf, the journey out of depression has involved learning to know and to love herself. "I wanted to very much, but I didn't," she said. "I would have loved anything, anybody in the world. And I was repeatedly told that you have to love yourself before you can love anybody else. And whenever I was told that by therapists or friends, I became very frustrated, because I would say, 'Doggone it, don't you think if I knew how, I would do it.'"

"Growing up, a lot of things went on that I didn't quite understand - a lot of pain and suffering that I didn't understand or know how to deal with and damn near killed me. I don't know all the psychological explanations. It may have been that there was, or is, a tendency toward chemical imbalance inherited from my mom. And maybe it was circumstance, or environmental. I don't know about the cause, but I do know that there was a sadness, a deep profound sadness, that I carried with me all the time. I could be laughing and having a good time, but let me come to a still place and that sadness was always there, a constant companion."

"So having carried that with me most of my life and having gone through the places that you go, and the people that you go to when you are looking for answers outside of yourself, I found myself at age 28, divorced from a man I had been married to for seven years and thought I would never be divorced from. And with that came the realization that I needed to choose a new name."

Amanda said she had learned at age 14 from an aunt who helped raise her that the man she thought was her father was not her biological father. "And I went and I asked my mother about it and my mom went to pieces, and I knew it was true."

"I learned at 14 that Manuel Metcalf was my father, and I proceeded to forget about it until the age of 28, faced with having to name myself. I knew that Grogan, Charlene Grogan, the name I had gone by all my life wasn't it, and in marriage I became Charlene Beal. Then with the advent of women's liberation, I became upset that I was a lawyer, in an office working with men who were all called by their last name. I was the only one they called Charlene, the women did, the men did. I was in this little short body – a small, petite body at that time - and I was really hell bent on having every bit of respect everybody else got. So I had them call me Grogen-Beal. I had hyphenated my last name with women's liberation at that time, and they kind of laughed it off. You can't really force anybody to call you anything. So I went home one night and I told my husband, if we ever have a daughter I am going to name her Sir Arthur Grogan-Beal. And he said, 'If you are going to do something like that, you do that to yourself, you don't do that to a kid.' And he was right. So I went down the next day, literally, and filed papers to change my first name to Cir – spelled C-I-R. I kept the C."

"And that next morning, he got up all wide eyed and he said, 'Look, you are all over the newspaper. Herb Caen, who was a columnist for the San Francisco Chronicle back in that day, had written an article about this Deputy Attorney General for the State of California who was tired of not getting enough respect. And because they wouldn't call her by her last name like they did the guys, she went and changed her first name to Cir. 'Cir, Yes Cir,' I went to work that day and nobody knew what to say to me. They were all wide eyed, and I walked down the hall, and somebody said to me, 'Charlene.' And I kept walking and they said, 'Charlene.' And I said, 'You don't have to answer to that anymore,' so I kept walking. And I heard this stuttering, 'Ms. Grogan-Beal.' And I said, 'Yes.' It was a very long drawn out way of getting to where I wanted to go. I think it represented a sense of powerlessness that I had always had and I think I wanted that recognition. It didn't bode well, because I made everybody called me that - my mom, my brothers and sisters, and my husband. Having your husband call you Cir was a little bit of an odd situation."

"We were separated about a year from that point and I don't think it was at all because of that. He was a very liberal minded man. But … in the process of trying to find out what I would call myself, I took my older sister to dinner and I said, 'I want you to tell me about my father.' And she ordered a double scotch, because nobody in our family was permitted to talk about that."

"She said my father was a short, roundish-faced man, with a very nice smile. And he was very nice to mom and the kids. But one day he was brought home by an uncle who was a member of the police force in this small, little town. They had a black police force and a white police force. So my uncle brought my dad home and he said, 'Charlotte, we caught him stealing groceries and I don't want to put him in jail. So he's either got to pay for the groceries, which he can't do, or he has to leave town.' He had been doing this for a little while. My mom thought he had been bringing home the groceries from work, but he didn't have a job and he wanted to save face, so he had been stealing the groceries and bringing them home. My mom was a real strict Christian woman and so the thievery didn't set well with her, so she bid him goodbye. And somewhere in the recesses of my memory, I think I have some smidgeon of a recollection of his being around me, but he left when I was six months old and I never heard from him again - not a card, not a letter, not anything."

"So when I set my sister down and she told me this, I immediately went home - and she said the last time we heard of him he was living in Chicago - so I called Chicago information and I asked for a Manuel Metcalf and they said, 'Here is the number.' I called and an older sounding black man answered the phone. I asked if he knew a Charlotte Grogan and if he had ever lived in Cairo, Illinois. And he said, 'I think you might be talking about my father; his name is Manuel Metcalf, too.' And as we spoke he said, 'They told me I had a sister out in California somewhere.' And we became close friends in the 20 years from that time forward until he died about five or six years ago."

"I never knew my dad. I asked my aunt for a picture at one time, but my father never took pictures. My brother asked me over for Christmas once and I told him I would really like to have a picture of my dad. I always felt like I would be a daddy's girl. Somehow all my life I felt that the reason my dad left was me - if I were loveable my father never would have left. Now, I know that makes no intellectual sense what-so-ever, but the child in me, the baby in me, that was the precise articulation: if I were loveable, he wouldn't have left."

"So being determined, which I got from my mom, to have some part of him, I learned that night that he had died when I was 16 years old and that he had come to California during the war and worked building ships in Marin County. Curiously enough, I had ended up in Southern California in the same small county in California where my father had lived. I remember the first time I came through the Golden Gate, that they had rainbows painted on that little tunnel that takes you to Sausalito and I just thought it was the most beautiful serene and tranquil place I had ever felt. Maybe he felt some of that too. But isn't it odd, that both of our lives, we would both end up in this county."

"So the difficulty, being a kid who felt that she was lost and not worthwhile and not loveable, and the long journey that it took me on. I named myself after my father. From Cir Grogen-Beal, I became Amanda Metcalf and changed my name legally —that being the closest to Manuel Metcalf that I could get. I took his surname and tended to represent him in the world. My brother, who I was told was very much like him, was the sweetest, most gentle man, and I just love him. We just loved each other the minute we saw each other. So coming from that point, going through a difficult divorce - which I had learned had more to do with my not knowing who I was, or where I was, or who I came from, or what I was supposed to be doing in life and having this deep sadness - I made a commitment to try to learn who I was and become who I was. And I remember the conversation I had with myself. I said, 'You know you are really kind of messed up. There is a whole lot that I think is objectively wrong with you.' And I said, 'A lot of people go through life with this stuff. They may not live desirable lives, but they get through. I think most people do just kind of make a peace with who they are and what they are and just go on. And if you are really gonna work with this stuff, and pull the scab off of all these wounds and hurts, there is going to be a long time. It's not gonna be a quick fix.' But none the less I said, 'Let's go do it.'"

"So I commenced to read a lot, and go through various programs. At one point I was looking to Werner Erhard and EST. I was reading a lot, doing a lot of metaphysical reading, and transcendental meditation, and just spending time with me trying to do the work. At one point Cecil Williams, who is a very good friend of mine and a minister in San Francisco at the Glide Memorial Church, I went to him because I didn't want to be with the law firm any more. I was tired of that kind of practice. And he introduced me to a man by the name of Jim Jones, who had the Peoples' Temple in San Francisco. I realized when I met Jim that he was a very charismatic man, he was something special, he was a mystical light. You couldn't deny it - there was an attraction, because being around Jim made you feel whole, made you feel loved. You honestly felt that by virtue of being around him you were getting what you needed that was missing. I got involved with Peoples' Temple trying to help the Temple because of bad publicity, and as a lawyer trying to use my skills. And the reason I have taken this offshoot from the story is that my pain led me to some often dangerous relationships and choices. After Jim left and went to Jonestown, we were still in communication. I would go up to the temple and go into the basement and there was a shortwave radio and we would be in radio communication with him in Guyana. I would give him reports about what I was doing, and Jim said, 'Amanda I want you to come down here.' And he said, 'There is another plane leaving next week and I want you to be on it.' I was to speak with him in another couple days and I said I would definitely think about it and let him know what I was going to do. I don't recall, but I think I had pretty much decided that I wasn't going to go, but I don't know why, when I turned the television on one night and got the news about the 900 people being killed in Jonestown. So was it that he was totally charismatic and anyone would have been seduced or induced to go there, or was it that I was in so much pain, that I was looking for love anywhere I could find it? I don't know."

"To wind up this story, I have persevered. I learned to know more about what I really wanted. I never thought I would be a woman without a man in my life, and because I made such poor choices, because of what I was trying to find in relationships, at one point I faced a truth. I said, 'Johnny and Billy and Paul, and Joe and Dick - what were the common factors? You, sweetheart, are the only single thread that runs through all those unfortunate relationships.' And what I realized, which was really hard, you are going to have to be alone, by yourself. No male relationships, because that messes you up because it takes you off, and you go searching for stuff that you don't need to be searching for there. And you are not ready to be a good mate, so leave it alone."

"So quite literally, for years I was voluntarily abstinent, after having been out there, I mean out there and having a lot of fun. I had to, because it was just clouding up everything else. And at one point I realized that whereas I thought I wanted the American dream - the man and the kids and the perfect family home - I realized that Hollywood had done a lot of damage. And a lot of the ideas women have about what is desirable really have no solid, spiritual or real foundation. It's way too much make believe and not in a good way. And as a part of what I came to understand was that what I really, really wanted, was to be OK with myself. That is something that I never thought was possible. I thought I might get the man, and the kids, and the house and the way of life, but to really love me and really be OK being with me - that was a bit farfetched. Except I realized on this journey that's what I got to be. That was the hardest thing: not loving myself, not knowing how to go about loving myself, and starting from scratch standing in the mirror saying it to myself. Taking the time, because there was no manual out there showing how to do it, from the basic caressing my own check to learning ways of being kind to me. I am really proud of that, because it is what has been the hardest thing and the most rewarding thing in my life."

When asked about the lies about herself or the world she had believed to be true, Amanda said, "Lie number one, that I wasn't beautiful. I remember when I was a little girl I asked my mom if I was pretty. And she said, 'It's not prettiness that counts, it's what's in your head that counts,' Now how kids interpret things, I said to myself, 'Ah, huh! You ain't got too much going on in the looks department, so girl you better be smart.' That's how I interpreted that."

"Also compounded with that was that I grew up in a very racially segregated area where not only was there racial segregation between blacks and whites, but there was really deep segregations within the black community. There was a color scale and it was epitomized in a phrase we used to say, 'If you're white you're right, if you're black get back, if you're brown stick around.' That was really true when I was a little girl."

"And so like most of the girls who I grew up with, I grew up putting bleach on my skin because I wanted to be light. My mother would say things when I was a little girl like, 'Get out of the sun, you are going to get so black I won't know you.' All those things that lead you to believe a lie, that you are not attractive. Watching Miss America and saying you know, 'That will never be me cause I ain't got the goods.' And somehow saying that was wrong. That was lie number one."

"Because of that lie, I believe I was led to be more attracted physically to – that's part of it - to light men. I was married twice and both of my husbands were white. ....Now I have come full circle and I can honestly say that there is no bias or preference on my part about the color of a man's skin. That has been a journey in itself. So I would say the first one was the lie that I thought I wasn't beautiful because I was black. Other lies that I told myself or that people told me.... I think I have always told myself a lie that I was weak. I have always perceived the accomplishments that I have as a result of having some false bravado that it really wasn't me. Something that I could turn on if need be, but it really wasn't me. Now that I have thought about it, I think that was a lie. I think I am strong. And that doesn't mean I am impervious to pain, or fear, or difficulties. But strong, as people have always called me, yah, I would have to say that is right."

"My mother was a very religious woman. She sent us to Sunday school, but she didn't go to church herself, because where we lived there was a lot of judgment going on about how you looked. People put on their finery when they went to church and my mother through that was bogus. She was a person of very modest means, but extraordinary. Literally, at times I remember when she had two dresses: one she washed and one she wore. They used to say she'd take off one cotton dress with a wrap around tie and put it in the washer and put the other one on, but every penny she had went into her kids. We always had whatever we needed. She worked different kinds of jobs in factories during the war. She worked in a hospital. She took in laundry. She cleaned homes. She did whatever she had to do, usually working two jobs because she had four kids. She instilled in me the importance of having a personal connection with God. So I went to Sunday school and watched my mom not go. I remember my mom had a statue of Buddha that she burned incense in. I don't know if it was just an ornament or if she had an attraction to Buddhism or some kind of Eastern philosophy. She was a kind of a mystical woman. I came out to California when I was 14 years old to go to school, because the schools where I came from were really terrible. And she came out the next year. She was in her 50s and so were her sister and her sister's husband, who came with. Because they were so isolated - I say because - they became Jehovah's Witnesses. Most of my family became Jehovah's Witnesses. I found it very far apart from the Baptist Church that I grew up in. After she became a Jehovah's Witness, no matter what I did - finish college, go to law school, become a lawyer, became a federal prosecutor, sit as a temporary judge, I did all these things – but no matter what I did my mom would always say, 'That is wonderful, but you still haven't found the Lord.'"

"But through the process that I was describing before, I said, 'Daggone it. You have not been honest with yourself. You have tried everything. You tried drugs, mystical seeking out the inner truth, all that stuff to get to some place that was higher or better. We thought we were looking for a higher place. I came from all of that, all the reading, and all the weekend seminars, and all the therapy sessions, and I was still in a really low place. I thought I had tried everything.

One day I passed a Baptist church. I really hated that my mom couldn't use scissors on Sunday. You couldn't make noise. You had to only sit and be quiet and reverent. So when I left home when I was 14, I never wanted to see the inside of a church. So my then-husband said, 'I heard this really great music coming out of a church in Marin City. You've always liked music. Why don't you go there?' So I went to the First Missionary Baptist Church and I took my son, who was about eight-months old, and I sat in the back. And the music was good and it was uplifting and inspiring. At one point the minister gave the call. But then he said, 'Have you told yourself that you've tried everything. Are you looking for peace of mind and you think you've tried everything? Well, unless you've tried the Lord, you haven't.' I said to myself, 'You don't just walk into a church and join, that isn't done.' But I said, 'Don't talk to me in the future about how much pain you are going through if you know that you haven't tried this means, this route, then just shut up cause I don't want to hear it anymore.' So I got my behind up and I went up in the church to join and I became baptized. And it was a really wonderful thing for several years. I was more focused in my business. I was more focused in my life and things went very well.'"

"About eight years later when AIDS was victimizing everyone, the preacher in my church went out after gay people as the horror, as deserving God's wrath and vengeance. He said AIDS was visited on them as punishment. My son's godfather was a man I loved very much. He was the best friend I ever had, a hairdresser from San Francisco who was just a wonderful, mild-mannered human being. He was dying of AIDS at that time. And I said to myself, 'Do I stand up and take these people to task or do I leave?' I knew I couldn't change their minds, so I left."

"And I experienced from that time on a kind of spiritual difficult isolation. I was doing personal battle with 'Does God exist?'- which I thought was a question I had answered long ago. I had been in an automobile accident before my son was born and it was bad. But in the course of that accident, I was tumbled over in the car several times and the car landed smash down on its roof. The steering wheel was even broken in two. And after the dust settled, I heard people running up and screaming, and I crawled through the windshield with the car upside down. I brushed the glass off myself and I felt absolutely wonderful."

"Now, I had way too much to drink, and way too much to smoke, and way too much everything. I got to the point where I was driving around curves fast on a one way street. And I continued to push the accelerator down and something said, 'If you don't take your foot off the accelerator you are going to crash,' And I knew that, and I didn't take it off. At one point I realized I had lost control of the car and the question came– in a real clear voice – do you want to live or do you want to die?' That had been preceded by many bouts of tortuous time spent alone thinking, 'God I want to take myself out of this.' At one point after my divorce I made a deal that if you stay with this one more year, and at the end of it, if you don't feel life is more bearable, I'll go with you. At the end of that year, I had to admit that I was still in a lot of pain, but it was better. So that option was gone. But I would stand out on my balcony, sobbing and weeping in pain, and a lot of serious depression, only to say to myself, 'Amanda, turn around and go inside. You are on the second story, you'll only mess yourself up. You're not gonna die!' That night when the car spun over and when I got out, people came up and a man came up and offered to take me to the hospital. There was some other intervention at some point, but anyhow I did go to the hospital …As the nurse was filling out her chart and as I was telling her the story of what happened, I sat bolt upright because I was telling her the story from the vantage point of a person sitting in the back seat. And I recall very vividly seeing my body rolling over and over, and a sweet soft voice, to this day unmistakable, the tone and the words, saying over and over, 'You are in an accident but you are alright.' Don't ask me how I know, but I knew that was my grandmother speaking to me."

"I never had a moment's pain. I was banged up and bruised. My brothers and sisters wouldn't let me go near my mother for a month because she would have fallen out if she had seen how I looked. But I went to work that next Monday after I took two aspirin. There was an epiphany. I really didn't want to die."

"What I would pass on to another human being is that we are spirit, much more so than physicality. And spirit and energy never die. I am not afraid to die. What I would say is establish your connection with God. Find out who and what God is to you. That is what is really important. Ultimately, I went to my mom when she was near death and said, 'Mom, I have found my own personal relationship with God. It's a relationship that get's worked on, but it has never gone away.' And she said to me. 'Yah, but you are still not a Jehovah's Witness.' And that was painful, because I will never be a Jehovah's Witness. And the fact that my mother could not say, 'Wonderful for you,' was a painful thing, but I had to learn to love her because she could not do that. Her unconditional acceptance and love was something that was not available to me. That was painful, but the wisdom that she imparted of connecting spiritually with the universe, that is where I am."

"So what I would pass on to another woman is love yourself and find your own connection with God and define it for yourself. ... In this journey there are some questions I don't want to have to answer again. So let's put this one on the decided side. There is a God. How I may refer to Him, or Her, or It, or call Him, or Her or It, that may vary. But there is a Spirit, if it's nothing more definite than the love of the universe, the Divine. Whatever words may be appropriate, that I know. And in times when I feel most frustrated or confused, I can refresh myself with the recollection of my own specific experiences where the Divine was kind enough to give hard-headed me some concrete evidence of His or Her or Its existence."

"The greatest joy in my life was the experience of raising my son. He saved my life at a time when I found no purpose in life, he provided that. When I was trying to learn to love myself, I remember his sweet little voice just saying, 'Mom, it's easy. Just love me. Just love me, it's really easy.' I don't feel I can elaborate. Finding my place in the world, no matter what else I may have done or may do, I am convinced that my calling was to be a mother to that boy. If I was put on this earth for a purpose, that was it. And my greatest joy has come through the experiences I have had, the courage I have found, the ability to keep on going, to persevere, to come back from the down and go back up. To understand and to know that tomorrow is another day, that there is a brighter side, that happiness is a state of mind. It's not where you are or who you are with. It comes from inside and if you want it, go get it, because it is always available to you. Those things I have learned in the process of mothering, parenting."

Johnnie Rose Rasmussen: The Dignity of Service

We met Johnnie Rose Rasmussen in Needles, California, heading west along the old, historic Route 66. Johnnie Rose has served diners in the Wagon Wheel Restaurant for more than 20 years. She is the daughter of Elva Paul Rasmussen and Melissa Louise Rasmussen, the mother of four children and grandmother to nine.

Johnnie Rose was born in Seattle, Washington and describes herself as a Navy brat. She described her road to Needles as a long story.

"My grandma and grandpa on my mother's side raised me from the time I was seven. I had my first child at the age of 17. The only reality that I had of what life was from my grandma and grandpa. My mom tried, don't get me wrong. But the only reality I had was from my grandma and grandpa."

Although life was difficult for Johnnie Rose growing up, her grandparents gave her a foundation that helped her throughout her life.

"They were good workers," she said. "No matter what happened, when things got tough, they would keep working. Times get rough, but you got to go on. You've got to get the shoes and the food and you can't be too proud to work."

"I learned from them that if you have to do dishes to get food, you do the dishes. It's not beyond you to do any work."

For Johnnie Rose, life's difficulties included facing the death of her own child. "I lost a daughter when she was in her teens. It was a bad time. You don't have reality with that one."

But it was her work that she claimed helped pull her through. "It kind of kept my mind off it and pulled me away from kids for a while."

"People say, 'You have other kids,' but the point is, you still have a loss. That was my daughter."

Johnnie Rose says it's the love of her family that she draws on for strength and support. "I have a grandson now who says I'm a sexy grandma! I draw on my son.

I have a granddaughter and I see them and they let me know they love me. And my mom is still alive and she says she loves me."

"I always saw why my kids did things. My girls, they got pregnant young. I was pregnant young. But you have to love them. In my grandparents day if a girl got pregnant young, they would send them off and send the baby off. But you don't do that. There is a baby there. There is something you can love. One of the girls here was saying something about abortion and some of the people were using it like a legal way of birth control. It shouldn't be. There is a fetus there. We are human."

For Johnnie Rose, her children have brought her the greatest joy in life and her proudest moments. "Probably one of the proudest moments was my son's high school graduation and making sure that (the children) got through school."

"For me, in my time and being in the restaurant business, we were taught cooking and ironing. But now I think kids need their education more. It isn't the same roles with a man and a woman. Now it is more important that you get your education and learn. We need to let our young people know to learn more. Women need to learn more than how is that steak supposed to be fixed."

"My most important advice to young women is to believe in themselves, not somebody else, but in themselves."

"The strongest hurt for me after my daughter died was that I remarried a man and I believed in him. But when it didn't work out, it really hurt me because I had believed in him."

"I think I have always believed there is a power stronger than where we are. There is something that happens when you lose a child. I think they are still with you because when things go real wrong and I go into it, everything straightens out. So whatever it is, they are still with you. You don't ever lose that child and you know they are at peace, because it gives you a peace."

"I remember that child and I loved each other dearly. I have talked to women that said they didn't know it when their child died, but I had a feeling and I knew it before we had even gotten the word. I just knew it. But there was a peace I felt because we loved each other. I believe there is something stronger and that is with her."

"I'm just a little woman, in this little town doing my best, trying to believe and trying to feed people. After all, people need to eat."

Truth

"Do the truth all the time. No lying. God knows what you do. So do the truth all the time."

—Connie Tooka Mirabal

Julia J. Curley: Living in the Navajo Sprit

Julia J. Curly was born at Grey Mountain, Arizona, near the Grand Canyon, the daughter of Frank B. Johnson and Grace B Johnson. She is the mother of six girls and four boys and is the grandmother or great-grandmother to 75 children. She is a custodian of the Navajo ways. We met Julia on a pull-out along the road to the Canyon, where she was selling her handmade jewelry. Julia is pictured here with her daughter Caroline Wilson. Julia spoke to us in English, although Navajo is her primary language.

Julia J. Curley was born and raised just outside the entrance to the Grand Canyon. "I was raised in this area. I have my dad and my mom here at that time. We don't have any car or truck or anything. All we have is wagons and we have sheep and horses. We were grazing on this area. We were raised on it. And my dad always go hunting for deer, and we were raised on that too," Julia said.

"At that time we had a big snow. It was really cold winters. Our days are not like that anymore. My mama used to do the weaving. That is where I learned from. They teach us how to raise sheep, horses, and how to ride horses. And we have cornfields and my dad was planting corn for the winter. And then we learned how to grind down the corn. We have our own grinding thing: that round rock. There is a little thing on top that we use for our hand grinding. But we learned."

"I am always learning myself. And the rest my brothers and my sisters are too. My dad taught us all how to do things. But now days it's not like that anymore; but still, my kids I teach them how."

Julia went to school, married and raised ten children. "I did all those things for my kids. And after that time there was no jobs. Nothing. I do my weaving, you know that, and get some groceries for them. And I work all this time for my kids. Now my kids are grown up. They married and taking care of their own kids now - my boys too. And I married to one man and he was working for the railroad for almost 50 years and then he passed away. He got cancer and I get his pension now days. That is what I am using to live."

Julia said it was the traditional teachings from her father that helped to sustain her during difficult times. "My daddy used to be a medicine man and he teached me how to do these things. He teached me what to plant, what you can use for your kids when they get sick. That is what I always use those. I am still using it. There are people that come around and ask me what kind of herbs that you using. I come

over with them on this mountain and I show them. We are still using those things. That is what we live on all these years."

"Then we have our own religion - to pray early in the morning and the afternoon, and the evening. We are still doing that. Myself, I am still doing that. So everything is OK with me."

As to advice to pass on, Julia said it is important that her traditional cultural ways survive. "Well, there are a lot of things I want to tell my daughters. What I want to survive is what my daddy gave me. I was telling his teachings. And to learn it. And to believe it."

She also wants her daughters to remember how to live off the land. "A lot of things I learned from them. Why we have a cornfield and some stuff in that. We used to have a lot of fruit on the mountain. We gather it up by this time. A lot of fruit and stuff like that for winter. I teach my kids that too. A lot of things that my daddy teach me, I teach my kids that and they understand."

Julia said that when she was 10 years old, she was sent off the reserve to school in Nevada. "They give me five years, but I didn't finish. I finished three years because one of my sisters got sick. My mom and dad were taking care of her, so I didn't go back. Mostly what I learned was from my dad. He went to school when he was young. And mostly what I learned from work, too. I didn't finish my school."

When she was young, Julia said her father always encouraged her to be strong. "My dad, he used to really help us when I was small. That time when we didn't have this road here. Right there was the old dirt road. That was the Model T road. And the first time, my daddy was working somewhere and he bought a Model T. And he would drive right back there in the mountains. And he taught us to get up early in the morning, so we get up and warm up that. It was a Model T but ourselves, we call it "Chitty." And he say go outside and warm up the Chitty. At that time they don't have keys. You have to go outside and (she made a motion of cracking) in the front. And here three of my brothers would be trying to start it. And then my dad comes out and says, 'What happened?' I don't know. It wouldn't start. Maybe it was too cold. So he goes over and gets the red ashes and puts it on there and he starts it. At that time it was really cold, you know. We had a big snow too."

"We had a hogan," she said. "You ever see a hogan out there on the road? Some of them are like this (fingers pointing up) and some of them are round. We live in it in the wintertime."

"At that time when I was small, we listen to our mom and dad really good. They tell us to do something, they tell us once. And the second time we get spanked if you don't do something fast enough. They chase you outside. They don't care if it's cold. After I got married, I had my kids. We were not rich. I just take care of my kids myself. And … I tell them go to school. And tell them go to boarding school. I still teach them when they get home to do some work at home."

"But we still holding our culture. I don't think they really going to never let it go. If we die, that will be. I don't know what happens. A long time ago, I used to have my daddy's side grandma. She was staying over there in the cornfield. So I was staying over there with them. And she always talked to me about how to live on the earth. This is the way."

"I used to work with the Peacemakers for 10 years, until last summer. We used to have a conference all different places, Arizona, New Mexico, California, Nevada. Then we all were working with judges, attorneys and all different Peacemakers. We all have different tribes too. The Hopis, the Paiute: all different tribes. They tell about always their own people, the same problems. We try to keep our religions. That is how I know some people and they all have problems. They have a hard time. I guess it's like that in the whole United States."

"A long time ago one of my great- great- grandpas, he used to tell a story. We are on the mountains picking pinyon. And they are gathering up all these—different people. We used to gather close together. And then he built a big fire and he was roasting the corn, dry corn. My old great-great-grandpa, he was sitting there. We all sitting by the fire and he always tell us, 'You are not going to be the same like this. We are not going to be sitting like this. Later on, you might see when you growing up and you get white hair, they are going to be a lot of things change.' And I was looking at him and I was thinking, 'How does he know all those things?' And I was thinking, I don't believe what was going to happen. Maybe he might see something. And he say, 'Way back, at the end, the kids they not going to be listening. They going to get in a fight. They going to hurt their mom. They going to hurt their dad. The last day you are going to see all the bloodies in the house; the mom's house and your dad's house and your family.' And I was listening to him when he was talking. And I was a kid and I don't believe him. How does he know everything like that?"

"Then I grow up and I was listening to that. I went through those things and everything come true, what he tell us. It's a true story and nowadays it's like that."

Julia said it has always been important to her to respect her traditions. "Early in the morning, I get up, go outside and pray. We are still doing. Maybe some of them are still doing. I guess some of the other people are like that too. They want to survive. They want to live a good way."

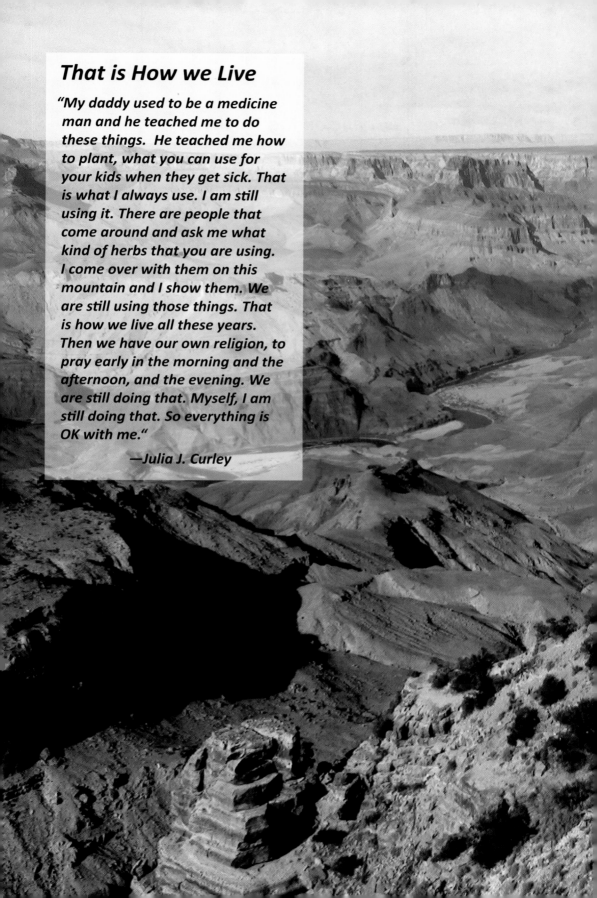

That is How we Live

"My daddy used to be a medicine man and he teached me to do these things. He teached me how to plant, what you can use for your kids when they get sick. That is what I always use. I am still using it. There are people that come around and ask me what kind of herbs that you are using. I come over with them on this mountain and I show them. We are still using those things. That is how we live all these years. Then we have our own religion, to pray early in the morning and the afternoon, and the evening. We are still doing that. Myself, I am still doing that. So everything is OK with me."

—Julia J. Curley

Caroline Wilson: Carrying on the Teachings

Caroline Wilson, Julia J. Curley's daughter, helped with the translation when we spoke with her mother. Afterward, concerned that her mother had not been able to share all she had wanted in English, Caroline began to talk about her mother and share with us some of what she learned from her mother when she was growing up.

"My mother refers to my grandfather's teachings a lot and the reason she does that is that a lot of the teachings came from him: more so from him than my grandmother. He was the one that was very compassionate with her when she was little, but who was also strong with her. He raised her in a way that was like, if she was being punished for something, he just didn't do it just to do it. He would explain to her afterward, 'This is the reason why I punished you.' He didn't do it just to do it, just to be mean or something. And that is why she refers to him a lot. He taught her how to shoot a gun, how to go hunting deer, how to skin a deer, how to butcher. She used to butcher a sheep in under 10 minutes and she would weave a rug. She wove saddle blankets. Surprisingly my grandfather got her the spindle that you make the yarn out of. And he taught her that she should get up in the morning and run towards the sun, to meet and greet the sun. He taught her how to pray - a lot of things that is just the person that she is. She is very compassionate, she is very kind."

"We live in an area that the land has been frozen for over 40 years. If you really look around, if you take a couple days and you drive around in this area, you'll see homes that have been depleted. People live in shacks. There are hardly any jobs. My mother had to work as a maid - clean rooms in motels, and things like that, to raise her children. She married my father in her early 20s and he was very abusive. She came out of that marriage and married another. The man that she later married really cared for her, and to this day, she – after he passed away - she lives on his pension. That is kind of a reward for her because in her early days she didn't have anything."

"To this day she doesn't live in a grand house or anything. She was supposed to be given a house by the Navajo tribe, but she allowed a younger family to take over that home because she said that they needed it more than she did. For her to raise 10 children on the pay of a maid, and then for her to allow her kids to go to school somewhere else, it must have been hard on her, but she did it anyway."

"The reason we are the way that we are is from her. She is just the strength that we look to. If you ask any one of my brothers and sisters, they will tell you the same thing. She has taught us to be good to people that don't like you. To pray for them regardless of how they treat you. You treat people as your equal, whether they are white, black or other nationalities. "

"She just teaches us that you have to do for yourself. You can't depend on other people, or the government, or your tribe because it won't get you anywhere. She teaches us to be compassionate towards other people when they need help – if you see other people that need help, you help them. You just don't look at somebody, when somebody is in need; you help them out. That is why when she says, 'If your grandmother or your auntie, if you see that they don't have any wood, you go get wood for them. Or you go over there and you chop wood for them, you fix dinner for them."

"These are the teachings that she taught us. Don't be greedy. Just little things like that over the years, because of the hardships that she has gone through in her life. She has kind of given it to us and we know what she has gone through and from that we have learned a lot, a lot."

"And I think we get a lot of the teachings from her instead of from somebody else. Some of us are traditional and some of us are Christians in her family. And she accepts that. I am a Christian more than traditional, and I respect what she believes and I respect the way she prays. And the way the family members are part of another religion, but I respect that."

"She is an advocate for children. She has her own child with Downs' Syndrome. She teaches us not to belittle other people because of their handicaps or the way that they are. Because it is a teaching that when you are given somebody like that, it teaches you to be compassionate towards people - to be glad that you are whole."

"Don't sleep late. That is one of her greatest teachings. Don't sleep late. Get up. Learn to do for yourself. Learn to do the traditional things. Make bread, fry bread. Butcher, plant, learn to do those things because in the modern days now you don't know how long those type of things are going to be around, because you are going to have to learn to live the old ways again one of these days. And so she just teaches us a lot."

"I go traveling with her other places and when I travel with her she just tells me stories. When she was a young girl, she tells me one story where her father, my grandfather, would tell her to get up before sunrise. And they didn't hobble horses then, they just let them go. She was only maybe seven or eight years old and he would get her up early and the horses would be maybe 10 miles away. It didn't matter that she was little or that she would get hurt running to get the horses, and she would. She would take off and she would run those 10 miles and she would find them and someway she would get on and she would bring them back. And then he would take the horses and hitch them up to the wagon and go get wood. She did a lot of things that men do, even though she was a woman. She was a sharpshooter. She can shoot a target like most young guys. They can't do the things she can. She is just unbelievable, the things that she can do."

"She is a great teacher. When you have Council, like you have chapter meetings, she will be there and she will be one of the main ones that will be saying things for her people. She knows what they need because she has lived in the area."

"Right now her grandkids have gotten together. Her children and her grandkids have gotten together and they are building a hogan for her, over where she keeps her animals. If you were going towards Cameron you could see it. It's really in a beautiful area. And they got together and it shows the love that they have for her - to be able to have a nice place like that to stay in. It is just her reward just having grandkids, I guess. She will have 75 this coming spring and they all love her. They just want to stay with her. They want to herd sheep for her. She has horses, so they come around and they ride horses. She still rides horses at her age. And she thinks she is still young. She still wants to do all these things that she did maybe 20 or 30 years ago, and it's getting to the point where she can't anymore. She gets aches, body aches and backaches and things like that, but she thinks she is still strong. And I believe she is, in spirit you know. Maybe not bodily, but she is in spirit."

"And she's always a teaching person. Whenever her kids or grandkids get together, she always has something to teach. And she tries to do it in English because a lot of her grandkids don't speak Navajo. And she goes out of her way to speak English to them. She will go back and forth between Navajo to English teaching them. Sometimes they understand and sometimes they don't."

"She teaches the way of the cradleboard. She teaches her granddaughters that you need to put your babies in a cradleboard. You need to do it this way; you need to have this done for them. Some of them do and some of them don't. It all depends on what they want to do. But that is just her way. She is a wonderful mother."

Success

"My life's greatest accomplishment: I hope it's not willingly hurting anyone."

—Jeannette Turton

Debbie Tafoya Trujillo: Love, Faith, Security and a Smile

Debbie Tafoya Trujillo was born in Winslow, Arizona, the daughter of Willie and Dora Tafoya. She now lives in Gallup, New Mexico with her husband, four children and six grandchildren. She teaches special needs children and is active in her Catholic church, where she was working as a volunteer when we met her.

For Debbie Tafoya Trujillo, faith and family are the most important things in life.

"I have two things that were really difficult that happened in my life and that was the death of my father and the death of my brother. My brother died when he was 31 years old and I was 19. They overdosed him on chemotherapy and that was really, really hard. I was in college and that was probably the first hardest thing that I ever dealt with."

"I never had anybody die in my family before and I felt that through my years up until I was 19 I was very, very religious. I always wanted to be part of the Catholic Church. I always wanted to be a CCD teacher; anything I could do for the church. When all of this happened, it was my parish priest that came and picked me up from college and took me to Tucson, Arizona and stayed with us. And it just showed me that they were behind me, that the Catholic Church was always behind me."

"But I think the hardest thing I have ever gone through was the death of my father, which was about seven years ago. My father and I are two of a kind. They even call me Willie."

"I just don't think that you can get through anything without religion - without your faith. And it was through my faith that I did get through it, plus the support of my husband. I don't know how people get through things without faith. You have to have faith."

"My Catholic faith, my mom, and my husband give me great strength and support. My husband is a great supporter: anything that I want to try, anything I want to do, he is right behind me, just right behind me, ready to help, ready to take on whatever I take on, together. He is a really big support."

Debbie said the proudest moment in her life came with the birth of her children. "It's absolutely amazing. At first I didn't think I could have children, but then at the birth of my son, even the feeling of him inside of me, it was just absolutely amazing. And then after that, having my daughter."

Just to know that she is a mother is Debbie's greatest joy. "I just love it. I just hold on to them very dearly. It is hard for me to just let them cross the street at age 13 and 15, but probably their births were the best moments of my life."

Debbie said her parents provided her a firm foundation of love and security. "I think I had a really great childhood. I know there are not a lot of people that can say that. I guess the greatest thing that my parents gave me was love."

"My mother never worked outside of the home. My father worked as a construction worker in the wind, and the rain and the snow and would bring that check home to my mom. My mom would take care of the bills and make sure the house was clean, and we were all taken care of. And he was a very strict man, but I knew if I needed a hug, he was there. And my mom was always there. I came home to a home and I didn't have to open the door by myself with a key. My parents were there."

"I want my grandchildren to know that. I try to teach my children that you've got to be near your kids. We coach everything we can coach, my husband and I, so that we can be near our kids. I try to teach my older sons that. Your kids have to always be secure with you near. That's probably it - love and security. I try and teach my boys, don't ever let your kids be worried that you aren't going to be right there. When they're crying, just say, 'It's OK, I'm here.' And get them to relax by that. But love and security is so important - and your faith of course."

For Debbie, the most important advice she can share is the importance of providing children a model of faith.

"Teach them your faith and love them. Know that they don't have to go to somebody else, that you are always open, that you are there for them, so that they don't have to look for somebody to talk to. And if they have questions, if you can't answer, go look for somebody who can. But you give them those answers from your heart and they will believe that. They will know that you are sincere. Don't let them go looking at other places for things. Be there for them. And if you have to say no and have to disagree, let them know it's still from love. It's from love, and you want them to be so safe."

As a teacher, Debbie said she learned another important lesson – the importance of a smile. "I have been teaching special education for 20 years and the one thing I do every single morning is I come in to my classroom with a smile. I might be the only smile they see that day and I think that is so important for these kids. You have to go in there and you have to show these kids that you care. And they will do anything for you, they really will. I walk into my classroom every day with a smile."

Education

"Education is so important. A woman without an education is a woman without a plan."

— Vera Earl

"When I went to college both of my grandmothers had a fit. But my father told them that I would be a better mother for it. And I firmly believe that. The nuns used to say, 'Educate a man and you educate a person. Educate a woman and you educate a family.' My father understood that."

—Jeannette Turton

"And the second (most important thing) would be to try and do the best that each person could in receiving an education. And that education could be in different ways, not all of it had to be scholastic where everyone went to get their degree. But if they didn't follow that route, which was an honorable one certainly to do, but to have some training in some field so that they would be able to work to raise their families. That was my heart's desire, and hopefully to a limited degree, I have been able to do that."

—Lauretta King

Dalia Vasiulis: Kindness, Art and Being True to Yourself

Dalia Vasiulis was born in Germany after World War II in an American refugee camp to Adolphus and Sophia Vasiulis. She lived and worked in the advertising business in San Francisco, California, before moving to Santa Fe, New Mexico, where we met her working in a downtown shop. She has one step daughter.

"Prior to being married to my current husband, I was married to someone else who died at a very young age, age 45. He was very, very sick and that was very difficult. When I was 18 my only brother died, also of a long illness. The most difficult times of my life have revolved around people I love dying - my parents, my whole family."

"I made it by just sheer survival, hope and wanting to be happy."

"When I was younger, I thought great wealth and great beauty were important. I thought great physical beauty, great popularity, those sorts of things mattered. Now I know that good health, knowing that I am a decent person, my husband, my pets, my garden, those are the sort of thing that really matter. The simple things in life."

"I can't really give any advice to young women, because I think that everyone has to find out for themselves. I really think that everybody is different. I think that everybody makes mistakes and they learn from their mistakes. But I guess the most important thing is to be true to yourself and to like yourself. I can't say I have gotten there, but I strive for that."

"What's helped me to get closer to liking myself is therapy! Just time, and age and learning how to forgive myself. Things like that. That's a real hard one. I don't think there was a great revelation, a great 'ah ha' turning point, but gradually, slowly it taught me some things. Things like trying to forgive yourself and kindness, which I think is very important. In fact going back to what advice I would give to younger women, I would say work on kindness. Do unto others, you know, that old adage."

"I do feel good about my relationships. I have had very good luck with that because they are so important to me, so I have had very good luck with that. I have been very good at loving, but that said, I still feel guilty for not doing that enough."

"My biggest regrets are that I wasn't nice enough to my parents; that's a big one. I still live with that. And I have a habit of working really hard. Like when my husband was dying, I thought to myself, 'I am not going to be able to feel guilty about doing anything wrong because I am being such a good wife,' but I still found things to feel guilty about. Like I should have done this, I should have done that. I did the same thing with my mother, a lot with my father, a lot with pets that died; that's my personal little flaw, guilt."

"I was brought up Catholic, so as you know a lot of religions are very rigid and dogmatic. Throughout the years, and throughout my losses and hardships, I sort of cobbled together my own morality, my own spirituality. And whenever I lose someone it gets stronger because I don't want to believe that there is nothing else. You know, I don't have a formula. I don't have any specific beliefs. I just have a belief that they are with me just because I want them to be."

Asked what she got from people she loved, or her culture that is important to continue, Dalia said, "I suppose I should think about these things a little bit more because I spend so much time thinking about what I didn't get. But I guess I got a lot of unconditional love from people. All those people put up with me and I appreciate that. My culture, my Lithuanian culture, gave me a sense of belonging, so it's being from some place. My husbands have loved me so much, I can't believe it."

"It's hard to give advice to young people because they are going to go their way no matter what. But had I, at a very early age, been less cynical and much kinder, and much more forgiving towards others and less judgmental, I probably wouldn't be struggling with a lot of the guilt that I have now."

"Before I moved here, I lived in San Francisco and I had one of those real heavy duty jobs. I was in advertising and that sort of thing, and, you know, I found that through all that stress and that necessity to survive that kind of world, you became a meaner person. And when I gave that up and I moved to Santa Fe, the stress left my life. I became healthier and I opened my eyes. I was less judgmental and less mean to people. When you are under that kind of stress and when you are in your 20's and 30's, boy, that so happens to you because you are trying to survive in the world. I have a step daughter actually and she lives in San Diego. She is 24 and she is going though that now. I just watch her. I can't give her any advice because she is going to find her own way, but she just stepped into that world as well. But she is a good girl; she is kinder than I was at that age."

Marriage

"Larry and I are probably each other's best friends. That's the most important thing in marriage."

—Jeannette Turton

Connie Tooka Mirabal: My Hopi Culture—It's All Inside

In many ways, the Women's Voices Project also began with Connie Tooka Mirabal, who, along with her husband Ernest, sponsored one of the first Spiritual Unity of Tribes Gatherings at Nambe Pueblo, New Mexico. A Hopi, born in Arizona, Connie was one of the few women we knew we wanted to interview and purposely set out to find on the journey. Her example of service at the Nambe Gathering was an inspiration not forgotten. While we found Ernest at their home in Nambe, Connie had suffered a serious stroke and was recovering with her daughter in Flagstaff, Arizona, where we caught up with her. Although her speech had been severely affected by the stroke and it was difficult for her to communicate, her spirit was as loving and bright as ever. Connie is the mother of eight children, three of whom died, 11 grandchildren and seven great grandchildren.

Connie Tooka Mirabal was born in King, Arizona in 1928 to parents of Hopi and Tewa descent. She wasn't raised to know the ceremonies of her people. "I just know it in my heart, from my family, parents. My dad was Mexican, Tewa, Hopi, and Aguada. He was mixed of different tribes, but he's Hopi and my mother is Hopi too."

Connie said one of the most difficult experiences in her life was the death of her father, who was murdered. "Someone killed him and we didn't know who. He was 84. And my mother she died at 84 also. That was really difficult."

Connie found the strength to keep going through all of life's difficulties through her faith in the Creator. When asked what gives her strength, Connie pointed upward.

"I know He help me. And now He help me too, when I got sick. I know He is here. He helps me and He heals me. So that happened and now I know that He is my father and my God. I know when you pray and ask Him to help, He do it."

"Oh yes," she said. "Praise Him. He gives us a life. And now I am 82 and I get a lot of advice yet. Sometimes He takes us early, but not me. He is busy when He wants us to do for Him, to serve him."

Connie left home at the age of 17 to go to work, and never went back. She married young and as a young mother had to raise her children by herself. "I tell you we didn't have a lot of money, but I get a new house for them. Somebody didn't give me things. I worked hard and made a life for myself and my children. I do it for my children."

Later, Connie met and married her second husband and her soul mate, Ernest, and moved away again, to her new husband's home in Nambe Pueblo.

"It was hard. But the same thing that they do, we do too. We pray, make a smudge to all directions. I do here too."

Now that she is a grandmother, Connie wants her grandchildren to learn the importance of honesty.

"Do the truth all the time. No lying. I say, God knows what you do. So do the truth all the time."

"Have things for yourself. You have to be able to do what you want to do. Do things for yourself, for your tribe, for your family."

Love

"The greatest thing that my parents gave me was love. I want my grandchildren to know that."

—Debbie Tafoya Trujillo

Audrey Deets Marcus: Art is a Gift from God

Audrey Deets Marcus is the daughter of Frank and Vera Deets, the mother of three children and the grandmother of three. She is a lifelong member of the Baha'i Faith, currently living at the Desert Rose Baha'i Institute outside of Eloy, Arizona. She is an artist who spent many years restoring murals at the holy places of her faith in Haifa, Israel.

Audrey Deets Marcus credits prayer as giving her the strength to overcome all of life's difficulties. "Prayer is absolutely necessary and we all know that, but it is amazing how it works. When everything goes bad, believe me you will say one or two. Then there will be a lull, because sometimes He's not going to answer right away. But eventually it will all straighten out. That's just how it works."

Audrey credits prayer for her being able to restore the murals in the bedroom of the home where the founder of the Baha'i Faith, Baha'u'llah, had been under house arrest in Israel. "After the Guardian of the Baha'i Faith* took over, he didn't have time to oversee every move that was made in relation to the restoration of the mansion. He knew how he wanted it to be, but there were some mistakes they made with the pattern in the walls, so they decided to do it over. It was pure white all around the rose windows. We started to put the designs back on exactly as they had been. And since I was the only artist at the World Center, I had the honor of doing that."

Audrey's most important piece of advice to give to her grandchildren is to obey the teachings of the Baha'i Faith and not worry about what happens. "If they meet people who don't believe, if they know the teachings then they will have the strength to do what is right."

---

*Shoghi Effendi was the great grandson of the Founder of the Faith. He served as its administrative leader in early years of the development of the Baha'i Faith.

When asked what the Baha'i Faith has meant in her life, Audrey cited her experiences growing up. "My mother was a Baha'i. And when I was about 18 I was attending art school in New York City and the war broke out - the Second World War. Before that the persecution of the Jews was very irritating to me and that was all we heard and I thought it was terrible. And so I began to read the books in my mother's house. She never pushed the Faith on us, but she had the books around —Baha'u'llah's books, Abdu'l Baha's and the Guardian's. I began to pick them up and read them and realized it was the absolute truth and there was no denying it. So I became a Baha'i. I think at about the age of 18."

"It helped me to live my life because it guides you all the time - what you should do in an emergency. And you have wonderful friends who believe the same way. And it opened up a lot of opportunities. I never would have probably gone to Israel if it wasn't for the Faith. It was actually my husband who was asked to go there. It wasn't me. He was asked to go to do the business-end of building the new Seat of the Universal House of Justice (the administrative body governing the affairs of the Baha'i Faith). And since I was an artist, Ruhiyyah Khanum** took a fancy to me. She was an artist also and she began to have a little more faith in me and a little more faith in what I could do. I had never done what I did eventually did, but I was given the strength to do it."

"My husband and I would always pray. I am sure most Baha'is do this, to find out which way you should go. Because you can go left, right and also you can get an answer, or think you have an answer, and often circumstances will change…. You have to think about that so you go back and forth for a while until it steadies and you realize, 'Yes, this is the way it should be.'"

"Well, there are going to be difficult times. We already see it and it is going to test all of us. And we will either get stronger or we will fail. It can go either way. I would say if the granddaughters have good grandmothers and grandfathers, that's a blessing and they can get strength from that. If they don't, God will still take care of them in some way and guide them."

"Some of the principles of the Baha'i Faith are the oneness of mankind, the unity of all religions. The oneness of mankind is important because there has always been the expectation that one day mankind will be unified and we are working toward it. Even now with the financial situation the way it is, everyone is beginning to realize that America needs help from Europe; Europe needs help from us, and England and France. And eventually they will realize that it's just one world. To be part of this, I find interesting; to realize that it has to be or we will fail—there are no two ways about it."

**Ruhiyyah Khanum was the wife of the Guardian of the Baha'i Faith and also one of its early leaders.

"When I became a Baha'i when I was 18 and went to art school in New York City, I was able to take my friends to Baha'i meetings and some very notable Baha'is were there. Dorothy Baker, an early member of the Baha'i Faith in America, was one of them and of course it influenced my life a great deal. For instance, one of the things in our Faith is abstinence from alcohol and if you are going to art school there is a lot of that being swished around. And you have to realize that for some reason Baha'u'llah made that a law. And you have to realize that one of the greatest evils in our world today is alcoholism. By being obedient, and not drinking, the principle of our faith helped."

The Spiritual World

"There is a spiritual life. That was the most important aspect of my life on this earth. Beyond the things that happen, we need to be in touch with the spiritual world, that side that makes us an even better human being. That would be the prime, important thing that I would hope to instill."

—Lauretta Walton King

Virginia Perkins Healy: Never to Stand in the Setting Sun and Hate Myself for the Things I've Done

Virginia Perkins Healy was born in West Haven, Connecticut, to Virginia Zott Perkins and Edward Francis Perkins. We met her at the Desert Rose Institute in Arizona also, where she works as a volunteer. When we asked her for a recommendation of someone who might be interested in being interviewed for our project, Virginia introduced us to Audrey Marcus. After some urging, she later consented to be interviewed as well.

Virginia Perkins Healy was born and raised in New England and says she adopted very basic New England values. "I was raised in the Congregational Church, which at the time I did not realize was a very liberal form of Protestantism, so the idea of having a relationship with God, the idea of being of service to other people, has always been important to me, as well as New England thrift. Basic human values.""Books have always been important to me. I have always done well in school and was at the head of my class, so the ability to think, to read, to solve problems and I think probably from this standpoint, being contented with what one has, are all important. Material things have never been that important to me or having a place in society. I think those are values from my childhood."

Looking back on her life, the most difficult experience she faced was when she and her husband almost divorced. "I became very ill. I had run a fever, not knowing it was stress. I was running fevers every day. My doctor finally said to me that my husband was very worried about me and he had run all the tests he could. And he said, "I'll make a deal, I will stop running tests if you will stop being sick.' And I said, 'O.K,' and that was the end of the illness. But the problem didn't go away."

It wasn't until a friend invited her to dinner that she found a solution to what was really bothering her. "My friend Wendi showed up at the place where I was working and she invited me to dinner. I almost turned her down, but I thought 'What the heck I'll go out to dinner with her. We stayed up all night talking and we became very good friends. At the time, when I needed to hear the words I needed to hear, Wendi said them to me. I was waiting for my husband to move, or make the change that was necessary to save our marriage. And I was the one who needed to make a decision or make a move. And Wendi said the right things at the right time, when I was ready to hear them. And our marriage stayed. At that time we were approaching our 17th anniversary. And we just celebrated our 44th."

Virginia said her faith, prayer and some very close friends are what she draws on for support during hard times. "I look to them for advice, for support to get me through and I try to do the same for them."

When asked if there was any advice she had for young women, Virginia cited a poem by Edgar Guest. "I am going to just paraphrase a little of it," she said, "but it starts out, 'I have to live with myself and so, I want to be fit for myself to know.' And later on it says, 'Never to stand in the setting sun and hate myself for the things I've done.' That's something I read in my youth and it has always stuck with me. Live your life, be true to yourself, know your values, don't sell yourself short, and as a Baha'i, I would add learn to be content under all conditions. I had an English teacher who always said, 'This too shall pass,' and I have found that is very true. Whatever the problem, whatever the trouble, whatever the good time, this too will pass."

Virginia's advice for getting to contentment was this: "I think part of it is prayer, part of it is attitude, part of it is reminding yourself that material things really don't matter. There was a man whose business burned and it was a lumber yard, and he was the chief employer in town. He was elderly and his friends all told him, 'Take the money, don't bother rebuilding.' But he said he wanted to rebuild because he was the chief employer and without his business people wouldn't have jobs. He said, 'So I have all this money; how many suits can I wear at one time? How much food can I eat for one day?' And I think that goes for being contented also. In trying to not be worried about things and in trying to not be upset about things, I find myself saying more and more, several times a day, the prayer, "God sufficeth all things about all things and nothing in the heavens or in the earth save God sufficeth. Verily He is in Himself the Knower, the Sustainer the Omnipotent." There are so many things we can't control and you need to be contented with what you have."

"The thing that is most meaningful to me is the fact that I have recognized Baha'u'llah. Why? Because we are spiritual beings. That is our reality, not our physicality. And I really believe that when we were in the womb we developed the tools we need for this world – arms, legs, eyes. In this world we need to acquire virtues, character. And those are the things that we work towards. The Baha'i Faith has given me a great deal, but mainly, it has brought me closer to God, to appreciate people more our differences and our commonality. It has made me see things in a different light."

"When you are young in some ways everything seems possible and some things don't seem very important. But as you get older your viewpoint changes and you wish you had the wisdom in youth that you finally acquired through suffering, through trials and tribulations. I would say to any young woman, 'Go for your dreams. Develop your capacity. You can be much more than you think as long as you don't let someone else hold you back."

Feel at Peace

"I feel really at peace when I can walk through the forest or along the river, along the bank. It is something I have always done, something I have always had a lot of opportunity to do. All of the things in nature we can't explain, I think that God gave them to us for a reason."

—Amanda Simms Donahue

Silvia Stoik Christianson: Respect, Choices, No Fear

Silvia Stoik Christianson was born and raised on a farm in Rice Lake, Wisconsin, the daughter of Archie Stoik and Hildur Andersson Stoik. She is the mother of nine children and the grandmother of 16. She currently divides her time between Delavan, Wisconsin and Coco Beach, Florida. She is the author's former mother-in-law and remains a life-long friend.

For Silvia Stoik Christianson, deciding to end a 57-year-long marriage was the most difficult choice she ever had to make. "I felt that I had a life to live beyond my large family and beyond my marriage. And I realized the only way to live it was to free myself from my marriage." Although making that choice and telling her nine adult children wasn't easy, for Silvia the pathway was the right one to take. "When I was thinking about getting a divorce, the decision was not done with haste. It was well thought out. I tried every avenue possible to avoid it – getting counseling and working for years on the relationship. But after I became ill and recovered from cancer, I came to realize that it was the right decision for me, despite what my family may have wanted."

"I read long ago when I was a teenager that if you are going to change people you have to go back and change the grandparents, if you are going to have a chance of changing the next two generations. I made the decision that I am going to do that - that the change is going to be with me."

Silvia said her life has changed dramatically since she decided to leave her marriage and take care of herself. "The freedom and good health I have now is unbelievable. When I first went into divorce I told myself some people are going to not like you, and that is the way it is. I went into it with that philosophy. But now I have so many friends and acquaintances and a rich extended life filled with interesting, wonderful people. We enjoy each other for our diversity. Some things I could never have dreamed of opened up. All sorts of joy opened up. I joined groups and my input is heard. It's like blossoming out."

"I took control of my own life and now I have the philosophy that if I get myself into a situation, I have always had the ability to get myself in the right direction. I just take care of things and just move ahead - no moaning and groaning. I just take care of it. I realized that I can just take an action; forget about what happened in the past and do what is necessary as the next step. I just move forward and don't dwell on things. You can always handle and take care of what needs to be done, go forward and continue living your life."

"When I was a young girl I was told by an authoritarian religion that if I took good care of my husband, he would always love and take care of me. I have found out that wasn't true. And I have talked with other women who have decided to get out of marriages and we all agree that is the biggest lie we were ever told. If you believe that you have to be with someone through thick or thin, you are going to sacrifice yourself and not be fulfilled as an individual."

"My ideas of relationships have changed 180 degrees. I don't believe that when you get married it is forever, because people change. Maybe you got in your relationship because of your hormones and the excitement of being in love. You should not be tied to that person. Maybe you married a lemon! It all goes back to respect. If the person you are with doesn't know how to respect you, there really isn't much to the relationship."

Silvia said the strength she has to face all life's difficulties came from her upbringing and from her ancestors. "My grandfather was in immigrant from Sweden. He had come to Barin County in Wisconsin in 1891and my grandmother followed in 1892, coming across on a ship with a baby girl, a five-year-old girl and a seven-year-old son."

Silvia said she knew that her mother always believed in her. "She wanted more for me, and although she often didn't know what to say or how to say it, I knew she wanted something more for me. And on my paternal side, my father and my paternal grandfather were very respectful of women. It gave me a sort of a strength and determination that when problems began to arise that I could not solve, in me somewhere was strength to go on. I think I was born with a strong sense of inner strength and knowing who I was. The support from my mother and father and the stories I heard about life before I came on the scene, as well as the respect of my father and paternal grandfather, gave me a sense of self respect."

Silvia said she now works to encourage and promote respect for oneself among her grandchildren. "I try to instill in them that they deserve respect, that they are unique human beings and they need to find out what is the special thing they are to do. If they can find what is special and unique to them, that will be the thing that will add to their whole life, to their family, community and to the world. Each of us has something to offer and that thing will add to the whole picture of what life is. If you can find that within you, then you will know what you can contribute to the whole world."

"I am proud of my children and proud of my grandchildren, because they took advantage of the opportunities presented to them. I encouraged my children and sacrificed so they could have piano lessons. At that time it was 75 cents a lesson, but there were lots of times when I had to go scrounging for that 75 cents. But I made the decision to get a better piano because I felt the training of their musical ear needed a piano that could stay in tune. I struggled for a whole year to buy a new piano. I could tell my children had musical talent, good voices and loved music, and that was to bloom and blossom and mature. I still have a son who plays piano and I have a lot of children still interested in arts, things they can do with their hands as well as vocal part of it. I feel a lot of pride in them and feel I had a little part in their success."

For Silvia, education and continual learning is food for life. "Read, listen to politics, learn about all kinds of different things. The most exciting thing for me is when I find out one new thing every day. Have a question. There is an answer. I just find that exciting to learn and ask intelligent people."

"Another thing I think is important is to do one good deed every day. Take out someone's trash, say hi to somebody, do a good thing and don't be afraid to tell someone you did it! When someone drops something and you pick it up, say, 'Now that's my second good deed of the day.' And they will smile and maybe that will be passed on to someone else."

"I always tell young people, if I see a young girl when she has performed, how much I really enjoyed their performance. I'll say something like, 'Do you know you have a lot of talent. Remember you have a wonderful voice and remember don't give up no matter what." I see the faces of people receiving a compliment light up like a 200 watt light bulb. It's important to let people know that there is something good about them."

"And I really think it's important to let your facility for humor grow every day. There is so much humor in the world. You just have to laugh and find the positive in things."

You Don't Need a Lot of Things

"Another thing I have learned is that finances have a place in happiness, but you really don't have to have a lot of things. I don't have to have brand name things or a big house anymore to be happy. I really think getting in debt and overextending yourself is a big mistake. Being in debt is very stressful and it can disrupt a happy marriage."

—Vera Earl

Darlene Johnson Nix: Knowing How to Serve, How to Cry, How to Love, How to Speak Your Truth

Darlene Johnson Nix lives part of the year in both Yuma, Arizona and Casper, Wyoming. One of 12 children born to Art and Mabel Johnson in Grandville, North Dakota, Darlene is the mother of two children and the grandmother of two. Both she and her husband, Fred, enjoy serving others and Darlene remains active as both a Hospice and community volunteer. We met Darlene standing outside of recreation center in her trailer community in Yuma and were invited back to her trailer for tea.

Darlene Johnson Nix is a short woman with a big personality and an even bigger heart. But throughout her adult life, Darlene had to face an obstacle common to many other women.

"Probably throughout my life, the one thing that may not be difficult for some people, but it was for me; is my size - my shortness," she said. "And so to overcome that you try to use more of your personality, or other strengths that you have, so people look more at that than your size."

At just under five feet tall, Darlene always aspired to being five foot three. "Size shouldn't matter, but it has mattered to me."

Being raised on a farm in North Dakota, Darlene never had much of an opportunity to travel as a young girl. "There were 12 of us kids, so if you got to go seven miles from town, you had gone a long ways. So I used to sit around and dream about going to a different state."

Darlene said her parents were "very, very poor people" and as a young child she believed money was the key to happiness. "I thought if you had money, it would be the answer to all things, and of course money is not the answer to all things."

Through her life experience, Darlene learned that the key to her happiness has come in service. "I do a lot of volunteering. My whole thing in life is to be able to help someone else and see them smile. I just know that I am in better health and better condition than they are, and I just love to help other people through volunteering. That is my whole focus since I retired. That is one of the things that probably would be one of my strengths."

Darlene volunteers with cancer patients in Hospice care. "I go visit the patients and take them whatever they need. Or I just visit them and hold their hands," she said. She also volunteers at a local hospital. "I visit one floor of heart patients to see what I can do to make their life better. And I'm in the Angel Program that also serves people with cancer, taking them a meal on the day they receive treatment or baking cookies and leaving them on their doorstep. I love volunteering. I just love it."

For strength and support in her life, Darlene draws on friends, family and God. "Sometimes friends are as important as family, because you can speak to things to friends that you don't speak to family, and vice versa. To me they are both very important, and that is where I get my strength to draw from."

"The main thing is that I just use God's strength to overcome difficulties," she said. "Death of family members to me is very, very hard to overcome. So I just ask God for strength to get through it. I recently lost my little auntie that my husband Fred and I have taken care of for years and years, so I just pray every day for God's help, and know that she is still here with us."

Darlene said the most important accomplishment in her life "was marrying my husband, because he is one in a million. When they made him they threw away the mold. So he is probably my best accomplishment, because I got him over anybody else."

And as for regrets, Darlene said her biggest regret is that there are people who have passed on that she wishes she had spent more time telling how much she loved them."Or just that I was maybe a little bit better listener than I was, instead of thinking about me, thinking about them."

"I would just hope that I never hurt anyone, because that is not what I'd like to do. But we all sometimes say things that are hurtful that we shouldn't have said. So I think that would be the biggest regret - if I hurt someone or if I didn't express my feelings better to them - particularly a dying person that I failed to tell them enough times how special they were, so that they could leave this earth knowing that they were OK people."

As for advice for the next generation, Darlene quoted the poet Emily Dickenson. "She always said, 'If in one day I could make someone smile today, then my life is complete.'"

"I think for our young people, no matter who they are, they need to know how to love someone. They need to know how to cry and they need to know that it's OK to express your feelings. Whether it be about politics or about life, they need to be able to express that without being fearful of being reprimanded for doing so."

As for maintaining a happy marriage, Darlene said the most important ingredient for happiness is what you are willing to give. "I just think that when you meet someone that you have to be willing to give 99 percent and only take one percent back. And if you can do that, or can see that quality in him, then I would say you found the right person. And first of all, he has to be your best friend. From there you can develop a relationship. And of course to me, honesty is a number one thing. If you can't be honest with each other then you just shouldn't be pretending thinking that it's OK when it's not."

"My husband is that type of guy," she said. "He gives 99 percent and I take one. And hopefully I return that. When you go into a marriage you have to know that you have to give and hope that you get the same back – but if you don't, then don't be disappointed. Take the one percent and be totally content."

And Darlene stressed that faith – no matter what religion someone practices - and hard work, are two other key ingredients for a happy life. "Hard work is so important. You mustn't be afraid of hard work. And it's important to be able to take advice from someone and use it as a growing tool, rather than getting angry. I think we were taught that, growing up."

Madeline Musengo Perry: Italian Cookies, Good Eating, Las Vegas and Engelbert Humperdinck

Madeline Musengo Perry was born on August 19, 1902, the oldest of nine children born to Carmella and Anthony Musengo. She currently lives in an assisted living facility in Agoura Hills, California. At 103, Madeline was the oldest grandmother we had the privilege of interviewing.

Madeline Musengo Perry was the oldest of eight brothers and sisters born to Italian immigrant parents. "My mother was born in Italy," she said, "and she landed at Ellis Island."

Madeline grew up in Chicago, where her parents eventually settled after spending some time living in New York. "My father had a brother and sister in Chicago, and my mother knew some families there that lived in her town in Italy."

Madeline said her parents always treated her well, but she always had to do things for herself and her younger sibling. "My mother didn't speak English. We worked hard."

The oldest of her eight brothers and sisters, she always had to help her mother. "I had three brothers one after another and there was a lot of whooping cough that went on those years. Somebody told my mother that those boys had to go down by the lake - that it would be good for their lungs. So I took my three brothers on the bus and we went down to Lake Michigan. Whooping cough was terrible. Then I had a sister five years old who died of pneumonia. It was so cold in the winter time in Chicago."

At the age of 21, Madeline married and started a family of her own. "In 1929 we had the stock market crash. Hoover was president at the time, President Hoover. He was a Republican. It was a bad stock market crash. We all had bought homes that year and we started losing them one by one, until Franklin Delano Roosevelt got in and he helped us all get our homes back. He helped us a lot, and I've been a Democrat ever since."

Madeline says she is fortunate to have a daughter, now 80, and a son, grandchildren, great- grandchildren, and great-great grandchildren. "When they come to me, I don't even know who they are, I said enough already, I can't keep up with them."

Madeline said the most difficult experience she had to overcome was losing all of her family members to death. "That's the hardest thing. My first grandchild died of cancer at the age of 39 and left three children for my daughter to raise. She had a wonderful husband, a wonderful home, three children that adored her. That gets me, why, why did she have to die? She was a good person. That was my hardest thing. Even though I did loose brothers and sisters, but grandchildren are closer."

When asked the secret of her longevity, Madeline couldn't point to any one thing. "I always was a good eater, but that's it," she said. "I enjoyed food. I kind of always watched myself, put a little weight on, take it off, put it back on again. I always made all my food. I made all the pasta by myself. I cooked a lot of sauce and gravy; I used to make Italian cookies. They went by the dozens."

"I drove my car up 'til I was 95 years old. I used to go to Las Vegas once a month. I used to go every month to go and watch Engelbert Humperdinck. He was my favorite singer. Although he was from England, he did have homes out here. I enjoyed his voice, I enjoyed his music. Whenever he would come out this way I made sure I'd see him. I was 95 years old the last time I saw him. He heard about it and he came down from the stage and he came up to me and he gave me a kiss! And he gave me one of those hankies he used to throw out to the audience and he made sure I caught one. And that was the last time I saw him, although I got a bunch of his records. When I went to Las Vegas, I was happy. I've got all kinds of pictures of him on my walls and magnets of him on my refrigerator."

Her favorite Engelbert Humperdinck song? "Please release me, I'm not in love with you. Let me love again, so please release me," she sang. "That's the song that made him. He tried everything until he sang that song."

Conservation Not Collection

"When I was young I thought that being rich was the important thing, but now I think that it's not the only thing. ...When I saw my parents in the hospital, I realized that material things cannot buy peace. People should focus more on spiritual things—on conservation, not on collection."

—Sonia Lee Chou

Mildred Keith Stark: Education, Reading, Expanding Your Mind and Never Giving Up

Mildred Keith Stark was born Nov. 3, 1922 in Chicago, Illinois, to Toby and Benjamin Keith. She is the mother of two daughters – one of whom is the author - and grandmother to five granddaughters. She was the middle child of five children born to her immigrant parents.

Millie Stark's life has been punctuated with tragedy. As a 17-year-old, she was in an auto accident while traveling with two teen-aged boys from her home in Chicago to visit her sister in Indiana. "I was sitting in the middle in the front seat in a brand new car. My mother hadn't wanted me to go, but I went anyway. I don't remember anything about the accident, but I was in a coma for three weeks and every bone in my body was broken. What else do you want to know?"

Millie had applied to a college in Illinois at the time, but the accident and subsequent years of recovery changed her life's direction. While the boys were thrown from the car and not injured, Millie went through the windshield. Her injuries were so severe that the doctors at the small town hospital where the accident occurred had virtually given her up for dead. Millie had glass from the windshield in her brain, severe internal injuries, the bones in her legs and arms were broken and her feet were severely crushed.

"By the time my mother arrived in Indiana, gangrene had set in my arms. But my mother insisted that I be treated. She had me brought back to Chicago and wouldn't give up. She insisted that I would live."

The year was 1939, and the surgery performed to remove the glass from her brain was so experimental, that the doctors who performed it never placed a plate over the portion of her skull that was removed. To this day Millie has a "soft spot" where the bone should be. "My mother was a sensational woman. She wouldn't give up. I owe her my life twice."

Three weeks after the accident, Millie remembers waking up from her coma in a hospital room and answering the telephone. Millie not only recovered from her injuries enough to walk again, but she went on to attend night school, work, marry, have two children and do everything in life the experts had said were probably impossible. And though she still suffers more than 70 years later from pain associated with her injuries, Millie pushed pain aside and never gave up experiencing life.

Millie's mother and father came to the United States from Lithuania and Latvia, respectively, and met in Chicago. The couple opened a small grocery store and butcher shop on the city's south side. Millie described her father as incredibly hard working and kind. "My father never let anyone go out of his store hungry. He was a reader. His greatest joy was to go to the park on the few days a year he closed the store, and read a book or a newspaper."

One of Millie's loves throughout her life has also been the love of books. "I love to read. My most important piece of advice to young women would be to expand their minds. They should read all the time. I don't think the world will survive without the minds of women."

Her parents raised five children during the Depression in apartments attached to their store. "My parents put in a false floor in part of the apartment, but the rest was concrete. My sister Shirley and I had the front bedroom. My brother and my sister, who was an infant, had a bed near the kitchen. My other brother slept in the hallway. We had 100 pound sacks of potatoes next to the piano in the hall. We all worked in the store after school. I never told anyone where I lived. I guess I was embarrassed. I used to have a lot of dates, but I would have them pick me up from a friend's house."

"My mother never learned to read or write, but she was a great lady. I don't have her strength. She could do anything. She was so smart that in her later life she used to advise my brother, who was a successful attorney. She could have been President of the United States if she had had the opportunity."

Not long after she recovered from her accident, Millie was struck with another tragedy. Her father was shot during a robbery in his store. Millie said she was the last person to see her father alive. "And I lost my sister, who was three and one-half years older than me. She died at 28 having her second child. I miss her to this day."

Millie went on to work as a proof reader at the Atomic Energy Commission. "I read manuscripts that the scientists wrote and would proof read them." It was during the Second World War and many of the manuscripts Millie read were classified documents associated with the work being done there to build an atomic bomb.

Like some of the women of her generation, Millie had a few engagements to boys who went off to war. "I didn't really want to marry them, but I wanted them to have someone to come back for."

But it was her marriage to her husband, Leonard Stark that brought Millie's life the greatest joy and the greatest meaning. "He loved people. He was very bright and had a photographic memory. We went to Europe many times and had a wonderful life together. What I want people to remember about me, is how happy I was with my husband for 50 years, and how much I miss him."

Expand Your Mind

"My most important piece of advice to young women would be to expand their minds. They should read all the time. I don't think the world will survive without the minds of women."

—Mildred Keith Stark

Ethel Nick Simpson: Just Do It

Ethel Nick Simpson was born in Cape Town, South Africa to Orthodox Jewish parents Isaac and Annie Nick. She is the mother of two daughters and the grandmother of four. She currently lives in a retirement community in Agoura Hills, California.

Ethel Nick Simpson was born to Orthodox Jewish parents in Cape Town, South Africa, and lived for most of her adult life in Rhodesia. She was raised with the strict traditions and values of her parents' religion, including keeping kosher and celebrating the Shabbat. "We just lived Judaism," she said. "It was part of me."

For most of her life, she has drawn on her mother for strength and on her mother's teachings in order to overcome life's challenges. "My mother was a very strong person. She passed away 18 years ago, so she was always there. She always knew the answers to everything. She would say, 'Don't fret. Take things as they come.'"

Ethel said her mother grew up "very, very poor and she built herself up. When something bad happened, she had the attitude, 'Too bad. Do the next thing, just pick yourself up and go on.'"

"When my mother was growing up she had to go to work and look after her grandfather. The family was in the country. When she was at school, on Fridays she would have to go home at noon and make the chicken for Shabbat dinner. One Friday she came back late and her teacher asked her why. My mother said, 'How can I tell the teacher I was busy cleaning a chicken for supper tonight?' She was really brought up the hard way, but those difficulties gave her strength."

Ethel said she also always worked. She worked in a bank and in a garage, or she worked helping out with family businesses. "My family was in all kind of business and I always went to help one of them in the shop. We had movie house when I was growing up, and I used to come home late at night on Saturday night on the caboose along with the train workers. The whole train would be locked up but my people got special permission to go on the caboose with the workers because we would get out late when the movie was over."

For Ethel, family was always the most important part of life. "We had an enormous family. If we had a ceremony we had to invite about 75 people before your could start inviting strangers or friends. It was an absolutely enormous family and we were very close."

Ethel met her husband at the beach in Cape Town and married at the age of 21, but not before she fulfilled one of her life dreams. "We fell in love and he wanted to get married straight away. But I had never been overseas and I really wanted to go. I told him he'd have to wait. And he did."

"It had been my goal all my life to come to America, but unfortunately for me I had to go via England and it make the trip that much longer. But I went with my mother on a thing called the See America Ticket: for 99 days for $99 you could go wherever you wanted. You could just get on the bus and get off the bus anywhere in America. It was 1962 and we started in New York, went to Niagara Falls, through Ontario to Detroit, Chicago, Iowa, Nebraska, Reno, Salt Lake City, Sacramento, San Francisco, down the coast to Los Angeles, to Las Vegas and to the Grand Canyon. I wanted to go on to Miami, but my mother said she was too tired. So we both went up through Dallas, Kansas City to Washington, D.C., and back to New York."

"After I fulfilled my life dream, I went back and got married and we moved to Rhodesia," she said. "I loved him. He was a wonderful, wonderful man – a fabulous man!'

Ethel said her most difficult experience in life was when her husband passed away suddenly of a heart attack in 1982. "I was just thankful that he didn't suffer and that is what sort of helped me over it."

Ethel said that while she isn't usually the one giving advice, she does have one important piece of life wisdom to pass. "Just do it," she said. "If you stop to think about it, you won't do it. I'm not a very decisive person because I think my mother made my decisions for me, she influenced me that way. But if I stop to think about - should I do it, perhaps I shouldn't - if I just get down and do it, it's done!"

She credits her brother's influence for pushing her along in life. "I have had my brother behind me, pushing me. He sponsored a lot of my trips and he kept me on the go all the time."

Although they weren't particularly close growing up, after Ethel went to Rhodesia and came back, her relationship with her brother changed dramatically. "He did something for me one day and I realized he thought of me differently than I had believed. My brother is a 'just do it' person. He built up business and still went overseas whenever he wanted to. He traveled the world and been absolutely everywhere."

Ethel said she has much to be thankful for in her life. "I've been very lucky. My brother has been wonderful to me and my husband and children have brought me the most joy in my life. I am very, very thankful."

Embrace the Medicine

"They say wisdom is lost. It's not lost. It comes in the wind. It comes all over. It surrounds us. It comes in our dream time. It comes in our hearts, in our blood. But because we walk upon the mother earth in a different time we forgot. But the tree has a voice. And the wind has a voice. And the star people have a voice. And the mountains have a voice. And the earth between us, underneath us has a voice. And all that is about has a voice ... And all we have to do is just open ourselves, embrace it. Embrace the medicine that the elders and the ancestors have to give."

—Adelina Alva-Padilla

Doreen Jacobs Roe: Education and a Fuchsia Bedroom

Doreen Jacobs Roe was born in Detroit, Michigan, the daughter of Betty and George Jacobs. She is the mother of one son and daughter-in-law, and has one grandniece. Her career was spent working as a nurse. We met Doreen while she was out walking her dog along the old Ventura Pier on a bright, sunny afternoon in Ventura, California.

Doreen Jacobs Roe was married to her first husband for six and a half years. She said she was very naïve at the time and didn't realize that he had an alcohol problem until it was very serious. "We had to end the marriage when my son was two," she said. "We were never enemies but there was this big white elephant in the living room that neither of us knew what to do with."

Doreen said she was a single parent for seven years, and never thought she would ever marry again. But later she met her second husband, a surgeon, to whom she was married for 21 years.

In her teen years, Doreen said it seemed to her she was so different from everyone else in school. "I was short and skinny when I graduated from high school. I was five feet tall and weighed 89 pounds. I was a stick. I didn't have any boobs and I had this curly, curly hair. And of course that was back in the 50s when everyone had these page boys and flips. I would put in these big rollers and by the time I got to the corner to catch the bus my hair was curly again."

"Parents, family and everybody would always say that I was cute. And cute to me was like, 'You're not pretty, but your face won't stop a bus either.' In my 40s I could look in the mirror and like the person I saw and not worry about those things so much. I won't say I don't worry about it at all, but I don't carry that burden around. It was a burden of my own doing and I really wish I hadn't put that on myself."

Doreen wants young women today to learn from her mistake. "Don't be so hard on yourself. Try to have the inner strength to say, well what those people are saying is not of value and it isn't true. It doesn't make me less of a person to not look like Reese Witherspoon or Paris Hilton. From somewhere find the inner knowledge that you are a good person."

Doreen said one of the proudest moments in her life was when she finished nursing school. "I had to leave in my second year in school because my parents had been ill and I had to go home and help them, and I didn't go back for 10 years. So it was a great feeling when I finished and had to take the boards. There were a lot of classes I hadn't taken for ten years and the state boards were two days and six tests. You had to score 350 on each of the tests to pass and when I got back the results I had scored 600 in three of the tests. It was a great feeling of accomplishment."

"I think it's really important for women to get an education. It makes more difference in your life than anything else. And it doesn't matter how hard it is. If you have to work and go to school and raise a kid, and still go to school taking one class a semester at night. Maybe it is an hour or two hours once or twice a week; but do it for your own self - to find out that you have the intelligence to do things. It changes the kind of life that you live."

"My education gave me the freedom to move from Michigan to Texas to California, and all I had to do was get a nursing license in each of the states and I could get a job within two weeks. Education is so important, especially for women. You can't move up until you have an education."

Doreen cited a nursing school instructor as one of the most influential women in her life. "As small as I was, she came up to my shoulder. She taught us humanity. She taught us to have a sense of responsibility to people. She taught us that nursing wasn't just a job, that it was important to be kind and to be nice to people. And sometimes it is important not to not be nice - because you might have to make a patient get up and walk when they don't want to. If you don't, then maybe tomorrow they are going to be in bed with a tube down them. She was an amazing example."

"Doreen also said the things she learned from her parents' example growing up also inspired her life. "We were all hard working responsible people because that is what our parents were. And it wasn't drummed into us, but we just saw them doing it every day."

Doreen said the birth of her son brought amazing joy into her life. "Every day it was a joy to be with that little infant and watch him grow." And she is pleased that her son absorbed some of his life lessons from her example. "I didn't find that out until he was 30 and I was 50 that every day he saw my husband and I going out and helping people and that he had those core values. We used to take old clothes to the Salvation Army and to the church, and we would give food. I think that's one thing we forget nowadays. Hopefully, the new administration will take us back to remembering that we are a cohesive group and that we are all Americans."

Doreen said it was also the values she learned from her parents and the support of her close friends that helped her get through the depression she felt after the death of her husband. "The year after he died was dreadful. I really didn't want to see other people. I didn't want to talk about it. I had to grieve in my own way. Because people have a tendency to say, 'You should do this, or you should do that.' But I had to grieve my way. But I guess it was the inner strength that my parents gave me, because they were strong determined people that started out with nothing, and just by living with them we learned to be that way."

And while she still feels the loss, she is learning to enjoy the freedom she has to face life alone. "My husband died when I was 60, and it was the first time in my entire life I lived alone. I bought a car on my own. I bought a house on my own. Now I have a fuchsia colored bedroom. I painted the house and every room is a different color. I go to bed when I want. I get up when I want. I really enjoy being able to do what I want to do when I want to do it."

"I am happy with my life. I think women need to learn that you can manage to squeeze it all in, but not at the same time."

The Spiritual Path

"So the ancestors, they are out there and they want to listen to us. Our strongest element is our voice. They want to hear us. They want to see our tears. They want to see that we know that they are still around, that we still embrace them with everything."

—Adelina Alva-Padilla

Donna Elam: Older Should be Bolder, Sing Like No One is Listening

Donna Elam was born in Santa Monica, California, the only child of Ardis Schulte Elam and Willis Blake Elam. She is the mother of one son, Daniel, and the proud grandmother of two grandsons. We met Donna while she was at work in a clothing and art shop in downtown Ojai, California. She agreed to meet us when she got off work.

Donna Elam has overcome many difficult experiences in her life, but the most difficult was ending a 17 year marriage. "It was a marriage that was never good from the start, but never-the- less I kept trying and trying," she said, "And finally I think I had help."

Donna said she and her husband were looking to remodel their home and decided, before they put too much money into it, to look around at other homes. "I found a house that I fell in love with and I went to the open house so many times that the realtor said, 'You've got to find a way to get this house.' So I brought my mother over and she fell in love with it too, so she said she would help us get it. I was married at the time and I was so excited. I was packing boxes and I kept talking to my husband, let's get going."

About two weeks before move in time, Donna said her dearest friend asked her for help. "She needed me to help move her mother into a rest home. She knew that if I was there her mother would be on her best behavior. I knew I was going to be back four days before the move and I had done all the packing of everything I could do, so I said, I'm going. My husband was very unhappy that I would put the needs of my friend before his needs, but never-the-less I went. And while I was there I got more insane calls from him and I realized, with the help of my friend, that this was my chance to leave if I was ever going to. If I had to move into the house, then it would be really difficult, so this was my chance now. And it has been a wonderful five years. I have blossomed. I have grown. It has been wonderful. I am so grateful, so grateful."

Donna said it is her wonderful circle of friends that have supported her through her difficult times. "And also journaling and reading, and just faith. I found a positive attitude is so important. I have always thought that, even as a child I realized that those people who were in concentration camps in World War II, how did they survive. Obviously it shows that attitude is everything."

For Donna, proud moments come in many ways, and sometimes even in seemingly silly ones. "I got up and sang in front of a bunch of people for the first time recently. I remembered a card with a saying that said, 'Dance like no one is looking, sing like no one is listening and live life like it is heaven on earth.' And I did that. I told myself that I was not going to go into that silly panic, stage fright thing. I was going to act like we were in the garage singing and having a good time and it worked - it worked. It was pretty amazing because I was a very, very shy child growing up."

"Of course having my son graduate from college, finishing my two year stint in the Peace Corps, and even though it isn't anything I did, it was still a pretty exciting and proud moment when my grandsons were born. And I guess I am proud that I did make that break and left that marriage."

Donna said she is happy every day that she can have a good attitude. "I work with the public and a lot of times women will come in. I sell art clothing and I love talking to them about not being afraid to show yourself. I remember listening to a program, like a monologue on late night TV one night, and an older black woman, I wish I knew who it was, said something that stuck with me and I use it all the time. I don't claim that I came up with it, but I use it all the time and I love to pass it on; and it's 'Older should be bolder. Older should be bolder.'"

Now that she is older, Donna said she realized that "keeping up with the Joneses, having that little tract home and the Lennox china - that's not important to me now. I like those things, don't get me wrong, but connection with people, just keeping your own integrity - those things are really important to me now."

As a young person growing up, Donna said she was fairly sheltered. It took traveling to Europe when she was in her 20s to open her eyes to all the ways people live in the world.

"I remember sitting in my rocking chair when I was little, and looking at the globe. I remember thinking, 'Oh that's my home, not just Long Beach, not just California. Oh, that is my home. It was something preparing me for later on and I really feel that way now."

Donna said when she was in the Peace Corps in Ecuador, she and a friend got a hold of a book by Krisha Murti. "We used to read and discuss it. When I got back home I showed it to my mom and she said, 'Oh, Krishna Murti lives right here, right behind you.' Her family had moved to Ojai, California and lived literally right behind the property where the famous Indian philosopher lived. "I got to hear him speak a couple times and I did literally walk from my mom's place to the meadow where he spoke. That was pretty cool."

The most important advice Donna has for the next generation of women is, "to take care of and respect yourself. Moderation and respect. I think we can go for a long time if we take care of ourselves. Don't let anybody put you down and have respect for yourself as you would have respect for others."

"And be comfortable with your body. Oh my God, if we only realized that we really are beautiful in all the variety that we are. I am sorry that we have these silly images that we have to live up to. Respecting yourself and appreciating the gifts that we have been given - it's amazing. Live life to the full and ask for help."

For Donna, meditation has been an important and transformational key. "For the awakening of your own dreams, I would say meditate. Sit and be still and listen to your inner voice. It is very important to be still, calm and centered and to listen. Relax. Listen to your inner voice. Listen to what is tweaking you - something will be coming to you so pay attention to your intuition. It isn't easy and it takes practice, but the wisdom of the ages is coming down. It is right inside of you."

We Honor the Earth

"We are Indian people. We have warriors. We have our people that we pray to. We have our lodges. We have our circles. We have the four directions that teach us the way it was taught to me. We are Chumash people. We are people of the western gate. We are the caretakers of the western gate. That is why our pole is black, for we are caretakers of that. And the south, they teach us it is the blood of our people and it is the site of the children and we take care of our children. And there is the white. There is the knowledge of our elders that is hidden inside of them, those stories. The ones with the white hair, the ones that carry the wisdom, the wisdom keepers. And then the sun in the east that teaches us to go out in the morning and embrace her and ask her to give us the energy to survive one more day. The beginning of life, the beginning of a new day. And then we honor the earth that is beneath us, for we are going to go back to the earth. And we honor the cloud people and the clouds that roam. And we honor the sun and the moon and the stars all over, for they take care of us. And we honor all that is around us on the earth for we are part of everything. We are only here for a while, and I am so happy to the ancestors that they showed me this way, that they embraced me, that they loved me enough to give me the gift of life."

—Adelina Alva-Padilla

Adelina Alva-Padilla: *The Creator is Good*

Adelina Alva-Padilla is the spiritual leader of the Chumash tribe of California. Born in Santa Barbara, California in 1936, she is the mother of seven, the grandmother of 36 and the great-grandmother of 34, "with four more in the basket." We met Adelina after we went searching for a member of the tribe whose traditional homeland was the Ojai Valley – Santa Barbara area, and were told to head to Santa Ynez. Waiting outside the Chumash tribal health administration building on a Sunday afternoon, a young man drove up to wait for other tribal members to join him for a presentation back in Ojai about the Chumash culture. When we told him what we doing, he immediately pointed to a home a few hundred feet from where we were standing and told us we wanted to speak with the spiritual leader of their tribe. He made a phone call and a few minutes later Adelina Alva-Padilla walked out to greet us and welcome us to her home.

Adelina Alva-Padilla has two last names and two fathers. "My step father is Patrick Martinez, Jr. and my mother's name is Juanita Salsa Kitano Pena. "Alva, which I now found out it's really de Alva," she said, "is my real father's name. Padilla is my children's name. My real father is Vincent de Alba. They spell it with a 'b' and I have it with a 'v.' They found me 15 years ago."

Adelina said overcoming the difficulties in her life has been a very, very long journey.

"From the time my mama left me with some strangers there were many, many difficult years. Even after my foster family and step dad's family was taking care of me, there were many trials and many things, from the time I came back at eight-years-old until I was going to be 17 and they married me off. By the time I was 22, I had my seven children. There were many difficulties. And what overcame my difficult years that made me put them in a bundle and put them in back of me and leave them there? Difficulties always hurt. They always touch your heart. And I think that is what makes you want to embrace the gifts that the Creator gives us, just to try to hug it a little bit more and embrace it a little bit more."

"I was drinking a lot and I was out there doing things I shouldn't have done. My young son was seven years old, going to be eight, when my husband left us. He had just gotten a wonderful job that was going to be more money, more everything… But when the sun shines, always darkness comes in. And he fell in love with someone else and left us. And so it was a very difficult time."

After her husband left and she was alone, Adelina suffered another trauma. "I had a stalker and the stalker mutilated me and raped me. I had moved because he threatened to kill my young son, so I moved to an apartment. While I was there, he broke the door and that is when everything happened."

Shortly after that, Adelina's mother was diagnosed with cancer. "So every day I would go and see her because she lived in the next town, Los Angeles. She would tell me to leave – 'You don't have to do this.'"

"She got worse and worse and finally three days before she died I was saying the Rosary by the window and she called me to the bed and she said, 'I made three headbands - one for each year that you will learn who the Creator is, who God is.'"

"I was still wearing tight Levis and tank tops and my hair was all ratted. I was hoping whatever happened, happened, so I could take my next drink." For three days Adelina's mother asked her to take the headbands.

"On the third day, the doctor called me into the office and said my mother was not going to last the night. As I walked into her room she told me, 'I made these three headbands out of shells. One for each year you will learn who God is, who the Creator is.' And she asked, 'Would you wear them?' And I told her, 'Yes.' It was the most wonderful thing that I think a daughter could receive."

"We brought her back to the reservation and they buried her. They sang her songs. They drummed. They drummed all night. And we buried her and I went back."

Adelina said she didn't think about the headbands until a few weeks after she returned home when she visited her dad. "'How do I look today,' he said. And I said, 'You look fine dad.' He asked again. 'That woman, she came to me last night and she sat on the bed.' I said, 'You are not supposed to have any woman in your room. You know the rules!' And he said, 'No, your mother, she came last night and she told me I was sick.'"

Although Adelina wasn't sure what to believe, she took her dad to see her doctor. "And the doctor said, 'Let's take him to the hospital. He's ready to have a heart attack.'"

"So I went to look for the headbands. I went to look for the little box where she said she had made these headbands. I went to go get the little box and I put the headband on and it fit. And so, for one full year, I went on a journey. It was a journey of where there was one bead and that represented me, and all the rest of them represented the rest of the people."

"So when I went back to work I took this - the first year – it was the bag of prayers. I went to work with my braids, my feathers and my headband and when I went in everybody was laughing. They said she's not going to last a week like that. The boss knew already, because I had asked permission to go back to work that way. They couldn't believe my pants were a little bigger, and my shirts a little looser, and no makeup. I had this empty bag that I carried with me."

"As the weeks went by I had this lady come up to me and she said, 'What do you have in your bag?' And I said, 'My bag of prayers.' 'No, what do you have in your bag?' And I said, 'Nothing.' And she asked me, 'Can I put my name there?'"

"Before I knew it, there were a lot of people and they asked me, 'Can I put my name in your bag of prayers. Before I knew it, I was dreaming about them and I knew exactly what they had. And I was wondering, 'What's happening to me?'"

"And then the spirits, they told me to make a hole in the bag and to make an altar. And I did and they told me that I didn't have to go to the cemetery to pray to my mother because she was all over, and all I had to do was to make a cross and I could pray anywhere, anywhere. So that was my year of the bag of prayers."

"And the second year - each year I learned something. And the second year was the year of the herbs. I learned that not all herbs were for me and that God, the Creator, was going to take care of the people and not me. But there were certain herbs that I would be able to carry and I would plant these. I would powder them and I would put them in an urn. …And I had to make everything part of me. And I had to touch it, and I had to hold it - part of me, part of me. And I used to take a bath and I would hold it and wash with one hand. Or pray and it had to be part of me. I used to sleep with it. So then I learned."

"So then came the third year. And the third year I learned to walk with the staff and be proud of who I was. And to be proud to the Creator and the ancestors, so they would take me to places I had never been. They took me to a lot of places. And I learned to be silent with my staff. And so, at the end of the year, the spirits came to me and the ancestors and they told me to go to the mountain. I went to the mountain and they told me, 'You bury your headbands, you leave your staff and your urn here in the mountains. And you go down the mountain and you will forget everything that you have learned. Everything will be erased and you will be the woman that you were. But if you go down with all your sacreds, you will follow me – and everything we taught you.'"

"But I accepted because during that time of the bag of prayers the stalker came back and he took me away to another place. But there was a purpose for it. A purpose when it was far to another nation. And there they took me to a sacred place that I still go to. Because when I got there to the entrance of this town, I turned around and I saw an Indian. He called me and I went there. And he said, 'This is yours.' It was a coat. It was something I still have and it looks like its new and it has been years. And he told me it will be alright."

"When they took me to this place, I saw the nine Great Chiefs of Gold in the sky. After I received this, the people used to sleep around the bed and I could never get out. And I remember that night the spirits spoke to me and they said, 'They will be asleep and you will come out to us and you will see us. So I looked up in the sky and the nine Great Chiefs of Gold and they all spoke to me. And they said, 'Each of us will give you a gift, a gift of life.' And the ninth one, when he spoke he said, 'When I speak again, get ready for your journey to come home for you have listened. And he told me, 'Tomorrow everybody will leave and there will be a man that will come and give you money. Then there will be a taxi. You go to the airport and you go home.' And it became so and I came home."

"And the journey began: the first year, the second year, the third year. Then they sent me to a journey up in the north in the mountains in California. And they spoke to me. And they told me that the journey would keep on going."

"I had an aunt in my foster family and she had a child - a woman - and she had AIDs. And when I stopped to see my auntie, she told me. I told her that every weekend I will come and clean your home. Her granddaughters were on drugs and her daughter had AIDs. And every weekend I would go and I would clean her house and then that is where I met my husband now."

"One day my uncle came in during that journey. My uncle was Yaki. He said this young man is looking at you. And I said, 'I don't need anyone in my life.' I had had it with men. My uncle said, 'No, he is a good man.' He said the man was outside and saw me throwing out the trash. And he said, 'Who is that young woman there?' And my uncle told him, 'Oh, she is an old chicken and if you put her in a pot of soup and you want to eat the meat, you cannot eat the meat. That's how old she is. But if you come and you sit with me for three years, I will introduce her to you because she needs to be treated good. She needs to be loved and she needs a lot of caring.' So he sat with my uncle for three years. And then my uncle said, 'He wants to take you to go meet his family.' And I went and I said, 'Oh my gosh, I don't want any part of this.' We went to a small trailer at a ranch. And I said, 'Oh my, all these people are outside and who knows who is inside.' But I went in and then I met his grandmother. His grandmother was in there and she was cooking. And she said, 'You are so beautiful. All I ask is you be good and just love my grandson. And so we have been married for 25 years. Her grandson is 45 now and I am 72. And he still loves me. He still cares for me. He ain't a perfect man, but he is all right."

"So the journey goes into my elder here. When I first came back to the reservation it was in the 70s. It was 1983 when I decided to stay. But the journey wasn't over yet, for it is the hardest thing to go back to your people, for they do not understand you, especially when you are speaking another language that the Creator has given you and your songs are different and your prayers. And you are not the person that you were, but you are the person that the Creator wanted you to be. I came back with my headbands. I came back with my dreams. Many, many trials. They didn't want me here."

"I would find my animals and I would bury them, but I stayed. I would walk the mountains and I would say, 'Lord, Creator, let me go. My people don't want me here.' But I would hear that voice saying, telling me in the wind, 'You need to stay, you need to stay,' so I stayed. And finally with many trials and tribulations - not that they really accepted me - but something happened. I had walked my talk with them, and so as I walked my talk something tragic happened and the council called me and asked me to be the spiritual leader of the tribe. And I said yes. And since 1994 I have been the spiritual leader of the tribe. And I try to serve my people well, for they are all my people and they are all good people."

"During the time of the bag of prayers and the urn and the staff, when they asked me to bury everything and leave it there on the mountain, I love that place of dreams, of hearing, of knowing that I didn't have to go inside a church. I didn't have to go inside a building. I knew the Creator that created the earth would walk with me if I believed. So when I came down with my bag of prayers, with my urn, with my staff, I walked down the mountain so proud because I was free - free from the little girl who was tied to a tree and raped every single day, free from the woman, that when I got my first job, I was raped and left there like I was nothing. I was free from everything that ever happened to my body. I was free because the Grandfather, the Creator of this earth, set me free to accept my bag of prayers, to accept the carrier of the herbs, the urn, and the staff that taught me to be proud."

"I was part of a tree - the tree that had roots, the tree that embraced the earth, the tree that had the trunk. And I was the trunk and my children were the limbs, and my grandchildren and my great grandchildren and all that was to come were the leaves that would fall from the tree and let me know that I was free."

"… And so I know that the Creator speaks to me, to everything that is in the earth and walks with me and every single leaf, every single tree, herb, and every single plant. And my ancestors, through the clouds make forms that I can see. I can see them. I come from the Bear Clan and the bear speaks to me. When I visited one of my elders - he was the spiritual leader of the tribe - when I went to visit him he told me, 'They will ask you to be the spiritual leader of the tribe and you accept that. And go to the Bear Clan and talk to them. And I told him they will not accept a woman because the Bear is danced by the men. He said, 'They will accept you. And bring the Bear Ceremony back to our people.'"

"On the first year that I took care of the ceremony, I went to visit the men that are the caretakers of that ceremony. My gift to the first man was Condor feathers, for it is very strong and it does a lot of healing. So I took the Condor feathers and I asked. I said, 'I want permission for you to dance for us.' And he took the Condor feathers and he asked everybody else, 'Should we accept them?' So for the first three years they came and danced and danced. ..And so now after the four years I brought the dance back to our reservation and they danced it for our people. Then I brought it here and I brought it here to take it away from the political place because it needs to be nurtured, it needs to know it is free. "

"My elder, our spiritual leader, he is in the spirit world now. He was and is a good man. He started all the dances here. He worked hard, very hard, to bring to his family the traditions, the ceremony, all that there is and all that there was. And the spirits they took him home and he is in the spirit world. But his legacy will be forever. My children say, 'There is a legacy with you, mother.' I don't feel that."

"From the time that we learn that there is the seed, and it travels and it travels and it has a lot of detours. And when we think we can't get over things, yes we can. The only thing that takes us there is the old ways of the people - the fire. And that fire will always burn as long as it burns in the heart of every Indian person and their spirit. Our mind can go crazy on us and take us in every different direction, but a heart, a heart knows loves. It just goes to sleep for a while, but it knows love. And that love needs to be nurtured and given. And that is what the fire does for us; that is what our traditions do to us. They bring it back and when there are hard times, we go to our fire. We go to that tree, to that wood we put in the fire and it brings all the stories out and it brings all the things we need to know. Our ancestors want us to acknowledge them when they appear in the clouds, when they appear in the sky or in the night. Or when the rain drops and we think they are crying for something. Or when the storms come and they are telling us, 'We send you the storms so you can learn. Know that if you ask us, we will be there for you.' There is no storm that we can't get over, no tragic thing that comes in our lives that we cannot override. For the Creator is with us and walks with us in everything that happens."

"When I thought that I was in the worst part of my life, when I thought that I was with the headbands - that it was over because I learned, I obeyed, I wasn't. But when the nine Great Chiefs of Gold appeared and told me, 'We will always be there for you. And when the ninth one speaks, get ready. Put your hair on the pillow so they can lay you down.' All these are things that they taught me. 'When I speak you start working and putting all these things together to come home.' It will be a good journey when I go home because I know that all of them going to be singing the songs. They told me the story of going home. My spirit will go to a special place where the salt water will wash everything away. Where I will travel across the spiritual river and the ancestors are singing the songs. And then they part and the Grandfather will come through and embrace me and tell me I have done good. I listened. I heard. I did it. I had this dream and I followed the dream."

"On the third year of the Bear Ceremony that my elder told me to do, I had a dream of this bear claw. I woke up in the night and I told my husband, 'I had this dream.' ... And the next day we woke up and we went to this ceremonial place and I walked up to my fire keeper and I said, 'Why do you have this fire keeper over there when you are the fire keeper?' And he said, "He asked me if I would teach him and I said you wouldn't mind if I did.'"

"So I go up to the new fire keeper and the first words out of my mouth I said, 'What's your occupation?' And he said, 'I am a tattoo artist.' So I just asked, 'Would you come to my home and would you do some tattoos on me because I had a dream?"

"When I went to New York for a premier movie where they used my songs, there was a lady there that I had met at a Sun Dance that I had supported for about 10 years. And her mother comes up and said; 'I heard that you never say no to elders.' And she said, 'Would you come to South Africa?' I left in July to go there with my grandson and my son to South Africa."

"It took me a month before I met the person that I was supposed to meet. His name Craedo Matu. When I went up to Craedo, he went ballistic and I thought, 'What did I have that I had offended him with?' It ended up that he came out and he said, 'This is yours.'"

"I was always saying, ever since I started, 'We are like a spoon in a pot of soup. We are only here so it don't get burned.' And he brought out a spoon that was in a little bag that his mother had given to him. And he told me, 'My mother, in 1932, told me to give this to you.' And me being human, I told him I wasn't born in 1932. I was born in 1936. And he told me, 'Don't ever underestimate the power of the Creator. For a thousand years before you are born he knows you are coming. My mother carried it with her and she made it for you. And she told me to tell you, you are the woman of peace and you will travel all over and bring that peace to people.' And that was my journey to South Africa. And I asked him how he recognized me. And he said, 'My mother said you will have a bear claw on your right cheek.'"

"So the ancestors, they are out there and they want to listen to us. Our strongest element is our voice. They want to hear us. They want to see our tears. They want to see that we know that they are still around - that we still embrace them with everything."

"… We are Indian people. We have warriors. We have our people that we pray to. We have our lodges. We have our circles. We have the four directions that teaches us the way it was taught to me. We are Chumash people. We are people of the western gate. We are the caretakers of the western gate. That is why our pole is black, for we are caretakers of that. And the south, they teach us it is the blood of our people and it is the site of the children and we take care of our children. And there is the white. There is the knowledge of our elders that is hidden inside of them, those stories, the ones with the white hair, the ones that carry the wisdom, the wisdom keepers. And then the sun in the east that teaches us to go out in the morning and embrace her and ask her to give us the energy to survive one more day - the beginning of life, the beginning of a new day. And then we honor the earth that is beneath us for we are going to go back to the earth. And we honor the cloud people and the clouds that roam. And we honor the sun and the moon and the stars all over, for they take care of us. And we honor all that is around us on the earth, for we are part of everything. We are only here for a while and I am so happy to the ancestors that they showed me this way, that they embraced me, that they loved me enough to give me the gift of life. For without them I'd be nothing again. I'd be that little girl. But I remember that each time that something happened to my body, I would run to the swing and swing as high as I could so that I could touch God. But now I know that he or she has touched me so that I can walk upon the mother earth with all the wisdom that they have given to me."

"Wisdom is not born at birth. They say wisdom is lost. It's not lost. It comes in the wind. It comes all over. It surrounds us. It comes in our dream time. It comes in our hearts, in our blood. But because we walk upon the mother earth in a different time we forgot. But the tree has a voice. And the wind has a voice. And the star people have a voice. And the mountains have a voice. And the earth between us, underneath us has a voice. And all that is about has a voice. The elements. We are part of that. And I am so happy that they chose me to be able to be, to be able to be a wisdom keeper. For the people that wish to hear and the people that wish not to hear. For the tears will always come, but that is how rivers are made - with the tears of all women in the world."

"The Creator is good, for he brings everything to us. He might bring us some hard times, but he gives us some good times. And all we have to do is just open ourselves, embrace it. Embrace the medicine that the elders and the ancestors have to give."

"When they tell us, the white man, your language is lost, your songs are lost. But here is a book. I wrote it and it is true. You will learn it. We forget that they are out there just waiting for us to wake up and listen to them and hear the songs. And believe in our dreams that they bring. And believe and enjoy the atmosphere of the world, the earth. For everything is still there."

Meditate to Awaken Your Dreams

"For the awakening of your own dreams, I would say meditate. Sit and be still and listen to your inner voice. It is very important to be still, calm and centered and to listen. Relax. Listen to what is tweaking you. Something will be coming to you so pay attention to your intuition."

—Donna Elam

Zahra Dabiri: Patience, Acceptance and Faith

Zahra Dabiri was born in Tehran, Iran. She came to the United States in 1989 escaping the religious persecution of members of the Baha'i Faith in her homeland. She is the mother of seven and the grandmother of 19. I met her in a Los Angeles restaurant. Zahra does not speak English, so the interview with Zahra was translated by her daughter, Fareshteh.

In a conference center filled with thousands of people in Los Angeles, the diminutive Zahra Dabiri stood out.

"One of her sons passed away from cancer when he was four years old," Fareshteh said. "My brother would be 43 years old now." My mom is saying, "Whatever happens, I shouldn't question it. Whatever happens is the will of God."

"You always have to be patient and whatever happens you have to take it for a good thing in life. Whatever Baha'u'llah (the prophet-founder of the Baha'i Faith) says, I try to do. Thanks be to God, I love."

Zahra escaped from Iran in 1989, walking over the mountains from Iran into Afghanistan with her daughter and youngest son. "We left the country with a camel and one week - me and my mom and my brother," Fareshteh explained on Zahra's behalf. "We didn't have any food or any hygiene and we suffered a lot, but she was very patient. She was supporting us even though she was 65 years old at that time, but she was supporting us."

It was the time of the Islamic Revolution in Iran, and the government stepped up its persecution of members of the Baha'i Faith. "It was hard times for the Baha'is and they would knock on our doors in Iran and say, 'We are going to just burn out your house.'" Fareshteh said. "She kept asking us to just pray and telling us nothing will happen. She is a very positive person - very positive."

"During the revolution some people just knocked on our door and she was so scared for our family, because our house was a big house and we had two doors in the front and in the back," Fareshteh said. "I don't remember because I was much younger, but my mom is saying that she asked all the children to just get out of the house the other way and she was holding the front door to not let anyone come in. We survived."

"We couldn't get a passport from Afghanistan to Pakistan," Fareshteh explained. "It took us 13 months to get a visa, and we were only in one room, with just a blanket and some basic things. But she was always saying that you just have to be patient, strong and pray."

Zahra was very young when she lost both of her parents. "She was only 12 years old. Her parents were Moslem and she was born in a Moslem family. But her uncle and her aunt were Baha'is. She was raised by her aunt in a Baha'i family and she declared her own belief in the Baha'i Faith when she was 15 years old," Fareshteh said. "The rest of her family, they didn't accept her as a family member once she became a Baha'i. Even her own brother wasn't talking to her for a long time because she was a Baha'i."

But Zahra said the Baha'i principles of the equality of men and women and the unity of mankind were important to her.

"Be strong in spirit and believe in God and Baha'u'llah and be happy in this life," Zahra said."Be patient and love all mankind. It doesn't matter what your religion is. Be strong in your faith."

Go For Your Dreams

"Go for your dreams. Develop your capacity. You can be much more than you think as long as you don't let someone else hold you back."

—Virginia Healy

Lakshmi Narayan: The Divine Is In Each of Us

Lakshmi Narayan was born in 1928 in the city of Bhaga in Bihar, India. She is the mother of one son, Umesh Chandra, and the grandmother of two, Chris and Michelle Chandra.

Lakshmi Narayan is well-known throughout her adopted home of Ojai, California, as the kind and gentle librarian at the Katrona Library.

Lakshmi grew up in the city of Bhaga, in northeast India. She is one of six children born to P. Ramaswami and Meena Pillar, early members of the Theosophical Society in India. "My father became a member in the early 1900s, and at that time, if a husband became a member, the wife automatically became a member."

"We believe that the divine is in each of us, and that the divine is in all life, including plants, insects, animals, birds, all life. The Theosophists believe that all life is one, no matter what religion, nationality, country, language. The divine we aspire to is already there in all of us."

Her parents' example of how to live became an important foundation for Lakshmi in how to live her life. "I was fortunate to be born to good parents. We were very fortunate growing up. My father was very strict, but kind and loving."

"He taught us not to pick too many flowers, not to brush down weeds and grass, but to be kind to all life. Growing up we had gardens, and flowers, and we had servants in the British days. My father stressed the importance of treating all people like our family," which was different from how much of India at the time viewed the world. "We had to be obedient, neat, speak politely, and treat people kindly."

Becoming educated was important to both Lakshmi and her parents. She earned her degree in geology and was the first woman geologist admitted to the Geological Survey of India, headquartered in Calcutta. She spent a year working in the field and then moved into a lab position as a petrologist, a job she held until the birth of her son, Umesh Chandra, when she chose to be at home.

Lakshmi said her marriage to her husband S. Narayanaswami was a marriage of love, not one of the arranged marriages so common to women of her generation in India. "I was actually introduced to my husband by my father. We were allowed to go out and see each other and get to know each other. My husband was a geologist who traveled all around the world, including Russia. He was Deputy Director General of the Geological Survey of India Airborne Mineral Survey. It was an important position in India. Although he wasn't a member of the Theosophical Society, he lived it. He practiced the principles of kindness and equality in his work and in his life."

Lakshmi said it was the death of her husband that spurred on her life's greatest turning point. "My husband's death was the greatest difficulty in my life. He died of a heart attack in the prime of our married life. He had just retired and we had built a beautiful home. The news that my son was getting married to an Irish girl had just come. We were so happy. We were planning to go abroad to England and to travel abroad together. I thought the world had come to an end when my husband died. He was not just my husband, he was like my parent, my lover - he was everything to me. When he died I went blind. I was completely lost."

It was out of the depth of her loss that Lakshmi turned to the Theosophical Society. "I was searching for a place and suddenly I walked into the Society one day without thinking and became a member myself."

"I would say the values of the Theosophical life and the Theosophists kept me going. They gave me all the encouragement and accepted me into their family. There were two young girls in their 20s who came to my home every evening to play music and sing. Another woman, a good friend, came in every day. She told me, 'Come out with us. Look out the window. If the door has been shut, you have to look out the window that has been opened. You can't change the past, but you have to move forward.' They gave me the strength to keep on going. We live in a world of dreams. You have to accept life and these are challenges."

After working as the head librarian for the Theosophical Society at the international headquarters in Chennai, India, Lakshmi came to the United States in 1978 to work at the Society headquarters in Wheaton, Illinois. "My son was in England when his father died, but he moved to America in order for me to come here. He wrote to Dora Kunz, the President of the Theosophical Society in America, and she invited me to come here and work."

It is in the little things that she can do in service that Lakshmi has found her greatest strength – love. "It's important to strive hard to do the best we can to help humanity. However small and insignificant a job may be, we should do it with love."

Lakshmi said that for many people today love has lost its true connotation. "Girls fall in and out of love all the time, but love is more respectful, more spiritual. In the world today fathers, teachers, priests are abusing children. That's not love. It is sad. I don't blame them, I feel sorry for them because they haven't learned love, kindness and duty right from childhood. We are all one, and we are all divine. If we treat each other that way, we are helping the world."

Despite being a librarian, Lakshmi says it's not book knowledge that teaches you how to love. "You have to do learn it from your experience. Don't forget to respect mother earth, our human friends, and all the other life around us. Look at yourself and see what it is you are doing each day. Look inside. What are you doing that is causing things to be taking place on the earth. Ask yourself, what have I done this morning? Did I speak kindly? If a friend is rude, don't retaliate. If you do, they may not ever know love and kindness."

"You don't have to do Herculean jobs. Even little jobs done sincerely, with love and appreciation – humanity needs that. People are suffering and dying, but we can show our love and sympathy and it will carry them and us to higher realms."

Elizaveta Gavrilievna Soboleva: A Goal From Childhood

Elizaveta Gavrilievna Soboleva was born in Hatassy in the Sakha Republic, one of seven children. She is the mother of three and the grandmother of four.

Elizaveta Gavrilievna Soboleva grew up in the Sakha Republic during Soviet times. "My mother and father were people who worked hard during Soviet times. They were very, very hard workers and they received a lot of recognition for that."

Elizaveta said of her family of seven brothers and sisters, three, including her, are in the medical field. "We all have families and children and all of our children are educated."

As a young child, Elizaveta dreamed of becoming a doctor. "I am very fortunate. I really didn't have difficulties in my life because I had a goal from childhood that I was able to achieve. The goal was clear. I wanted to become a doctor and I became a doctor. Even if I was born a second time, I would choose the same field."

"I have had many proud moments in my life. Graduating from the university and becoming a doctor and birth of all my children were some of the highlights of my life. My parents are still alive and recently we were able to celebrate their golden anniversary, and that was a very proud moment as well."

While Elizaveta has no regrets about her career, she said she wishes that she would have spent more time with her husband and focused more on family life over the years and less time on her career. "I would advise young women to pay more attention to their family life, and not focus solely on their career."

"I don't have any regrets though. I think we shouldn't have regrets because we all learn from our mistakes."

As a doctor working with seriously mentally ill and alcoholic patients, Elizaveta faces head on every day some of Yakutia's greatest difficulties. "I can see from my work experience in the medical institute, how difficult it is for those with alcohol problems. Many of the men we treat have lost their jobs and their families. They have lost everything."

"I think that life has changed a lot here. For example, the political structure of the country has changed a lot. During the Soviet era we were going toward communism and now we are all going to capitalism. These changes have caused problems in our society. Every day on television, radio and everywhere we see all these commercials that give a distorted view of life. People don't have the ground under their feet anymore. I think that is partly why we have so many of these problems now."

"My advice is that people should treat each other with respect and respect each other. You need to have a certain attitude toward people, as if they are you. You need to have this kind of attitude toward everyone. It's important not to think of people as beneath you."

"In my work I see people who are alcoholics, who come from the street, who have lost their jobs and often they have nothing. But I try to remember that they used to be someone's father, someone's beloved husband. They used to be respected people before, and I try to always give them that same attitude of respect."

An Attitude of Respect

"In my work I see people who are alcoholics, who come from the street, who have lost their jobs and often they have nothing. But I try to remember that they used to be someone's father, someone's beloved husband. They used to be respected people before, and I try to always give them that same attitude of respect."

—Elizaveta Gavrilievna Soboleva

Akulina Vasilievna Vinokurova: Family and Love Give Women Strength

Akulina Vasilievna Vinokurova is from Srednekolymsk in the Sakha Republic (Yakutia). She is the mother of three children and the grandmother of five.

Akulina Vasilievna Vinokurova described her parents' marriage as a love story that has lasted a lifetime. "It was interesting to know the beginning of it," she said. "They used to write each other for three years. Each of them has a bag of letters that was sent by each other. When they would meet each other in person, they were so shy they wouldn't even hug each other. But after three years, they decided to marry."

Akulina was the first and only child for five years before being joined by seven other brothers and sisters. "I was the first and most beloved child in the family. I was the eldest daughter in my family and most important thing for me was that I tried never to hurt my parents."

"My grandparents lived together for some 50 years and they had a very happy life and a lot of children. My great-grandmother survived being alone in the tundra and there was a big wind storm, but she survived. And after that she married and she had six children and she was very happy."

"In our family our mothers and grandmothers used to be the heads of the family. Our fathers used to hunt and provide food for the family and they had the same status. They were the head of the family too."

"We really love our children and we were brought up in a family that had a lot of children. We used to take care of them. My mother is 81 years old now and still she likes to see her great grandchildren. We are all like that. When we see these little children and they smile, and everything becomes beautiful again."

Akulina said she has three brothers: one is the head of the Emergency Ministry, another a policeman in a village and the third works in the administration of the region. "My sisters are all doctors or medical workers. I have three children of my own. My son works in one of the shops with cars, one of my daughters works as a policeman and the other daughter is a student studying economics. And I have two granddaughters and three grandsons."

The most difficult experience in Akulina's life was the loss of her third child, who died at the age of 19 months. "It was a very difficult moment. He was placed in a hospital and was there for 30 days but nobody could save him. When he died it was the most difficult moment for the whole family. For two years I suffered a lot. I think the most important thing in that period is our family stayed together and we supported each other. And I worked a lot from the morning till the night and it was healing."

"We always visit his grave every year, and it has been 19 years since he died. Every year we go there. Now I have a grandson and his name is Damir, but sometimes I call him by the name of my son. It is very interesting how you react to that after all these years and you still remember everything."

For Akulina, family is the most important thing in life. "The couple should understand each other and support each other at all times. And the most important thing is love. If you have this feeling and you are loved, women get strength from this. And it is very important that people understand each other and love each other very much in all situations."

Akulina's happiness and sense of accomplishment also comes from her family relationships. "I am happy because I met a wonderful person and he is my husband. We never quarrel or argue. It is really wonderful to have this kind of family life when you both feel happy. And of course I am proud of my children when they achieve some heights in their own life. I am very proud of them too."

The Sakha culture of hard work and respect is an important tradition to pass on, Akulina said. "I advise my daughters to be industrious, to respect other people, to love other people and to love and respect Mother Nature. And it is important for them to learn to be able to forgive other people's mistakes and not to focus on other people's mistakes, but to be able to forgive them and to love them."

"I hope that they will stay in touch with nature and I hope that they will understand how important every moment is in their life, so that their days will be full of meaning. I wish them to meet their beloved husbands, to marry wonderful men and to have happy family lives so they will live to the moment to have their own grandchildren. I wish them to be happy too."

Akulina said she also wants her daughters to remember their family life growing up and learn from the mistakes of others. "They should try to avoid the kind of mistakes we made in our lives, and move forward."

"I think we come here to become mothers and grandmothers, have good accomplishments in our lives, beautiful family lives and to build our families with good works."

The Divine is in All Life

"We believe that the divine is in each of us, and that the divine is in all life, including plants, insects animals, birds, all life."

—Lakshmi Narayan

Anna Pavlovna Pavlova: Work Hard and Love Each Other

Anna Pavlovna Pavlova was born in the Sakha Republic (Yakutia) in 1920. She is the mother of 10, the grandmother of 17 and the great-grandmother of seven.

Anna Pavlovna Pavlova was born in the Sakha Republic (Yakutia) in 1920. Her parents weren't educated, she said, but were incredibly hard working people. "They hunted and had their own cows. They were members of the first collective farm that was organized in this Republic."

Anna said she herself didn't have much formal education, but "I had a wonderful life. I don't think of myself as having had really difficult times in my life. Even though the times of the Second World War were difficult, we were very supportive and industrious. We worked a lot and that is how we survived during those difficult times. We didn't have enough food or clothing, but we worked very hard."

It was important to Anna to educate her children to be hard workers and good people. "I had 10 children. Out of them eight stayed alive and now I have six of them. Their upbringing was due to the times. I tried to educate them to be industrious and wonderful people."

The greatest difficulty Anna had to overcome was the death of her children. "One of them, my daughter, died when she was 50 year old. My son died when he was 35 years old. I think that is the most difficult times, when you lose your children."

"I think one must have a very strong will to overcome these kinds of difficulties. And of course the children that are left, they help a lot. You can't say 'They died and I want to die,' because of course life must go on. You draw support from your children and the fact that you want something beautiful, and you expect something beautiful from your life in the future."

When asked what she was proud of in her life, Anna said she sees pride as a bad quality in life. "But the happiest moments are the successes of my children and the fact that I taught them to become educated people. All of them are educated and good people, and I think that is the most wonderful thing."

"And when you have children and your children have their own children, and those children have children – every time you become happy."

"My advice is that you all become good people, that you work hard, have families, educate your own children and to be supportive to each other and to love each other and to lead a peaceful life. That is my advice."

Difficult Times for a Whole Generation

"The war time was very difficult for us and that is why my mother died very early. But those were difficult times not just for me, but for a whole generation."

—*Avgustina Egorovna Pavlova*

Avgustina Egorovna Pavlova: Creativity is in our Genes

Avgustina Egorovna Pavlova was born in Olekminsk in the Sakha Republic (Yakutia). She is the mother of five children and has 10 grandchildren ranging in age from 26 to eight months.

Avgustina Egorovna Pavlova was born in 1939 and has been married for 50 years.

"I married a man from Suntarski Region and soon we will celebrate our golden anniversary," she said. "I am the happiest grandmother because I have accomplished all my dreams in life."

Avgustina said her father went to fight World War II when she was a young girl and came back in 1947. "He went into battle. The war time was very difficult for us and that is why my mother died very early. But those were difficult times not just for me, but for a whole generation."

"I was young, but I remember the support we got from the Americans. They gave us sugar cubes that as soon as you put them in your mouth, they would melt right away. I remember it was wonderful to have support from the Americans."

"During the war, all I would think of was eating something and I just wanted to get full. We had a family that had cows and not many people had cows at that time. Most of the people were hunters. Because my dad had a cow, we had warm milk and cream. All our family was very united and supported each other."

Avgustina said her mother gave her eldest daughter to another family during those years to become educated. "Those were difficult years. We drew our strength from our grandmother. She used to sew everything. She could sew fur hats and fur coats and fur boots. She was very famous in the village and of course she was the one who helped us a lot."

After her mother's death, Avgustina went to live with an older, married sister. "I finished school and I went to the Agricultural Academy. Not long after that I went to the Suntarskiy Region and I later became an accountant. All my life I worked as an accountant."

"The Soviet time after the war was very enthusiastic. It was nice because there was no famine and we had enough food to eat. We also studied a lot."

Avgustina said her grandmother's creativity was passed down to her family. "You can find artists and a lot of people who are very creative. It's in our genes. My youngest son is a designer and all my children have the ability to create beautiful things."

"Of course I am very proud of my children," she said. "All of them became good workers and most of the children are highly educated. I am very proud and happy of the success of my children."

"My husband is a very good man, too. We lived a very happy life together. He worked in the collective farms. Of course, we were brought up in Soviet times and our upbringing was in the Soviet way."

Avgustina said when she was a young woman, at one time she wanted to become an actress and she spent some time studying at the Institute of Culture. But she came home, married, and has never looked back with any regrets at her life choices. "The most important thing in someone's life is his or her children. If you have children, when you become old you are very happy."

And Avgustina believes that being truthful, resourceful and responsible are the most important values to pass on.

"I like traveling very much. I don't sit in one place. I like going to the national summer festivals. I read newspapers and I am interested in life. People should value their lives and the lives of other people. And the most important thing is that they shouldn't be greedy or jealous. They shouldn't think that other people have a better life."

Expect Beauty

"Expect something beautiful from your life in the future."

—*Anna Pavlovna Pavlova*

More Words of Wisdom for Our Daughters

"The Sakha tradition of keeping silent should perhaps change. Maybe it's not good. I think it's time to change. It's too hard to keep to yourself. You should share with other women - it will be easier to live." —*Tatyana Martynova*

―――

"When I became a grandmother, I felt a different way. I feel that the sun is different and the world is different. I have something new in my life. It was the greatest moment. —*Elizaveta Aleksandrovna Ivanova*

―――

"When I think about the lessons I have learned in life, I think that you can't be too quick to make decisions. You have to think things through. I wanted to marry to get out of the house when I was young. I knew I couldn't afford a college education, so getting married was my ticket out. But I realized that's not the answer. You have to plan your life. You have to have some sort of a plan and not just jump for one thing or the other." —*Vera Earl*

―――

"I've tried really hard to be a good teacher, mother and grandmother. If I have any advice to give to the next generation, it would be to be patient. Don't be afraid to keep on learning. Don't be afraid to admit mistakes. Don't forget to vote. Pay your bills on time and learn the perils of debt. Love each other. And have fun!" —*Jeannette Turton*

―――

"The most important aspect of my life on this earth is that there is a spiritual life. Beyond the things that happen, we need to be in touch with the spiritual world, that side that makes us an even better human being. That would be the prime, important thing that I would hope to instill in the next generation." —*Lauretta Walton King*

―――

"But my sister Kendra came down and found me on the streets and reached out a hand. She told me 'I care.' I realized that I was tired of the way I was living and decided I really did want to live again. I realized that I need to live for myself and for my kids. Now, I am in the treatment center and coming here to get help. I want to live." —*Larissa Williams*

―――

"When I saw my parents in the hospital, I realized that material things cannot buy peace. People should focus on more spiritual things - on conservation, not on collection." —*Sonia Lee Chou*

"All of the things in nature we can't explain, I think that God gave them to us for a reason. I think we have misused them - our trees, our fish. Our water is being polluted everywhere, not just here." —*Amanda Simms Donahue*

———

"For me, I hate to say it, I never did like romance very well at all. I have always messed up my romances, so far - but friendship I have always done well. I have had long friendships. There is some song that says 'I could never stand without my friends.' That is how I raised my kids. That is how I did anything and still to this day it is about community." —*Ann Matranga*

———

"Times get rough, but you got to go on. You've got to get the shoes and the food and you can't be too proud to work." —*Johnnie Rose Rasmussen*

———

"My daddy used to be a medicine man and he teached me to do these things. He teached me how to plant, what you can use for your kids when they get sick. That is what I always use. I am still using it. There are people that come around and ask me what kind of herbs that you are using. I come over with them on this mountain and I show them. We are still using those things. That is how we live all these years. Then we have our own religion. To pray early in the morning and the afternoon, and the evening. We are still doing that. Myself, I am still doing that. So everything is OK with me. " —*Julia J. Curley*

———

"She just teaches us that you have to do for yourself. You can't depend on other people, or the government, or your tribe because it won't get you anywhere. She teaches us to be compassionate towards other people when they need help – if you see other people that need help, you help them. You just don't look at somebody, when somebody is in need; you help them out." – Caroline Wilson

———

"It's hard to give advice to young people because they are going to go their way no matter what. But had I, at a very early age, been less cynical and much kinder, and much more forgiving towards others and less judgmental, I probably wouldn't be struggling with a lot of the guilt that I have now." —*Dalia Vasiulis*

———

"Do the truth all the time. No lying. I say, God knows what you do. So do the truth all the time." —*Connie Mirabal*

"There is a poem by Edgar Guest. I am going to just paraphrase a little of it, but it starts out, 'I have to live with myself and so, I want to be fit for myself to know.' And later on it says, 'Never to stand in the setting sun and hate myself for the things I've done.' That's something I read in my youth and it has always stuck with me. Live your life; be true to yourself; know your values; don't sell yourself short, and as a Baha'i, I would add; learn to be content under all conditions." —*Virginia Healy*

———

"Prayer is absolutely necessary and we all know that, but it is amazing how it works."
—*Audrey Deets Marcus*

———

"Read, listen to politics, learn about all kinds of different things. The most exciting thing for me is when I find out one new thing every day. Have a question. There is an answer. I just find that exciting to learn and ask intelligent people."
—*Silvia Stoik Christianson*

———

"I think for our young people, no matter who they are, they need to know how to love someone. They need to know how to cry and they need to know that it's OK to express your feelings. Whether it be about politics or about life; they need to be able to express that without being fearful of being reprimanded for doing so."
—*Darlene Johnson Nix*

———

"I drove my car up 'til I was 95 years old. I used to go to Las Vegas once a month. I used to go every month to go and watch Engelbert Humperdinck. He was my favorite singer." —*Madeline Musengo Perry*

———

"My most important piece of advice to young women would be to expand their minds. They should read all the time. I don't think the world will survive without the minds of women." —*Mildred Keith Stark*

———

"I remember listening to a program, like a monologue on late night TV one night, and an older black woman - I wish I knew who it was - said something that stuck with me and I use it all the time. I don't claim that I came up with it, but I use it all the time and I love to pass it on. It's 'Older should be bolder. Older should be bolder." —*Donna Elam*

"And when we think we can't get over that, yes we can. The only thing that takes us there is the old ways of the people - the fire. And that fire will always burn as long as it burns in the heart of every Indian person and their spirit. Our mind can go crazy on us and take us in every different direction, but a heart, a heart know loves. It just goes to sleep for a while but it knows love. And that love needs to be nurtured and given. And that is what the fire does for us. That is what our traditions do to us. It brings it back and when there are hard times we go to our fire. We go to that tree, to that wood we put in the fire and it brings all the stories out and it brings all the things we need to know. Our ancestors want us to acknowledge them when they appear in the clouds, when they appear in the sky or in the night. Or when the rain drops and we think they are crying for something. Or when the storms come and they are telling us, 'We send you the storms so you can learn. Know that if you ask us we will be there for you.' There is no storm that we can't get over, no tragic thing that comes in our lives that we cannot override. For the Creator is with us and walks with us in everything that happens." —*Adelina Alva-Padilla*

———

"And at one point I realized that whereas I thought I wanted the American dream - the man and the kids and the perfect family home - I realized that Hollywood had done a lot of damage and a lot of the ideas women have about what is desirable really have no solid, spiritual or real foundation. Its way too much make believe and not in a good way. And as a part of what I came to understand was that what I really, really wanted was to be OK with myself. That is something that I never thought was possible. I thought I might get the man, and the kids, and the house and the way of life, but to really love me and really be OK being with me - that was a bit farfetched. Except I realized on this journey, that's what I got to be." —*Amanda Metcalf*

———

"You always have to be patient and whatever happens you have to take it for a good thing in life." —*Zahra Dabiri*

———

"It's important to strive hard to do the best we can to help humanity. However small and insignificant a job may be, we should do it with love." —*Lakshmi Narayan*

———

"My advice is that people should treat each other with respect and respect each other. You need to have a certain attitude toward people, as if they are you. You need to have this kind of attitude toward everyone. It's important not to think of people as beneath you." —*Elizaveta Gavrilievna Soboleva*

"And the most important thing is love. If you have this feeling and you are loved, women get strength from this. And it is very important that people understand each other and love each other very much in all situations."
—*Akulina Vasilievna Vinokurova*

———

"My advice is that you all become good people, that you work hard, have families, educate your own children and to be supportive to each other and to love each other and to lead a peaceful life." —*Anna Pavlovna Pavlova*

———

"The most important thing is someone's life is his or her children. If you have children when you become old you are very happy." —*Avgustina Egorovna Pavlova*

Epilogue

The Women's Voices journey has changed me in profound and unforeseen ways. I had to face my fears and let go of any perception of control in order to travel the path. The journey meant relying on a Higher Power to guide me and trusting that I would meet the next right person, find the next right thing, or realize the next right step needed to complete this project.

Not only did I meet the right people, but the women I met were each inspiring in their own way. They were ordinary women like me. But they were also unsung heroines, facing their lives with dignity and grace. They taught me love, they taught me trust, they showed me humor and their experiences enriched my life.

In Ojai, California, where I had the blessing of spending several months writing, I was surrounded with the beauty of creation, warmed by the generous spirits of the people, and inspired by the creative energies of that special place.

When I returned to Alaska to make money to keep on going, I was blessed by a job and even more blessed to be supported to continue writing when I felt like giving up. In January of 2010, I went to my boss, Peggy Brown, and expressed my concerns about not being able to finish the book and work. I realized I could live with this project never being successful at all, but I couldn't live with myself if I didn't finish it. I owed that to the women who had taken the time to be interviewed and to share their lives so openly and so generously. Peggy supported my dream, allowing me time to face my obstacles head on.

So once again I set off in my Honda CRV, this time more sure of my ability to maneuver the car ramp onto the ferry, and started south once again, acutely aware of facing my fears of both failure and of success. And once again, the miracles began the moment I let go – friends gave me places to stay to write, helped with editing the video, and people appeared to provide help, support, kindness and healing. Miracle after miracle of God's grace poured forth the moment I let go and let God!

I learned that it truly is the journey, not the destination that makes life so rich and so complete. I learned that money and jobs had a way of appearing when they were needed and when I trusted in the Creator to provide. I never starved, I paid my bills, I met my obligations, and I learned the joy in living simply.

I learned to accept help – something I had previously found difficult and even somewhat shameful. The lie I believed to be true was that I could and should be "independent." I faced the lie head on and found a greater truth in how incredibly interdependent I am with all that is.

I learned to trust. I trusted God, I trusted my instincts. I trusted the messages that came in answer to prayer and meditation. I faced my demons of insecurity and learned that security comes only in freedom from fear of not enough.

I went from feeling sorry for myself for one failed dream, to feeling humbled and thankful for the realization of another. My marriage had ended in divorce after 32 years, but a new life opened up before me. It was a life I never could have had in the marriage we had created. In the unraveling of the knotted ball of yarn that had become my relationship with my ex-husband, I found the strand that was mine and mine alone. I learned to own what was mine and to let go of all I had carried that didn't ever belong to me. The burdens lessened and the pack I carried became lighter indeed.

I learned to let go of my children, Joy and Sarah, and to rejoice that they were adults whose lives really could and should go beyond their lives with me. I learned to love them as adults, as strong and independent women whom I respect and admire for the people they have become. I learned to better appreciate and respect more fully my mother, Millie Stark, for her strength and perseverance though all of life's difficulties.

I learned that the wisdom of the grandmothers surrounds us. To hear it, all one has to do is ask. I learned that it is in the quiet of those who wait to talk, that wisdom speaks the loudest. I learned that no matter how much society, institutions, ideologies, organized religions, governments or armies wish to silence it, the wisdom of the grandmothers will always prevail because it is born of love itself.

As I sit at the end of the Women's Voice journey, I learned that the most important prayer I can offer is the prayer of thanksgiving. I am so thankful to the Creator, to the women I met, to those whose support has come forward, and to those who will continue to come forward along the way. I rejoice in the journey, in the service, in the difficulties and in the sunshine of the spirit that has embraced me.

My prayer is that all who read this book will be emboldened to follow their own path, enlightened in their despair, enriched in their sense of who they are and embraced by the love and the beauty that surrounds us. My prayer is that the voices of all women will be heard throughout the world, and that as we listen we will heal not only ourselves and future generations of women, but our mother earth as well.

*A portion of the proceeds from the sale of this
book will go to support a
Women's and Children's Center in the
Sakha Republic (Yakutia).*

Thank you for your support.

*To order copies of this publication and to see
short video clips of the interviews with some of
these women, please go to
http://www.WomensVoicesProject.com*